WORM

Also by Mark Bowden

Doctor Dealer

Bringing the Heat

Black Hawk Down

Killing Pablo

Finders Keepers

Road Work

Guests of the Ayatollah

The Best Game Ever

The Finish

WORM

THE FIRST DIGITAL WORLD WAR

MARK BOWDEN

Grove Press UK

First published in the United States of America in 2011
by Grove/Atlantic Inc.

First published in Great Britain in 2012 by Grove Press UK,
an imprint of Grove/Atlantic Inc.

This paperback edition published in Great Britain in 2013
by Grove Press UK, an imprint of Grove/Atlantic Inc.

1 3 5 7 9 8 6 4 2

A CIP record for this book is available from the
British Library.

ISBN 978 1 61185 584 5

Printed in Great Britain by CPI Group (UK) Ltd,
Croydon, CR0 4YY

Grove Press, UK
Ormond House
26–27 Boswell Street
London
WC1N 3JZ

www.groveatlantic.com

For the inimitable James M. Naughton, aka, Swami, who in a typical moment of inspired whimsy thirty years ago, named me "science writer."

CONTENTS

PRINCIPAL CHARACTERS

T. J. Campana, Senior Manager for Investigations for Microsoft's Digital Crimes Unit. He now works out of Microsoft's Redmond, Washington, campus, and was the primary representative of the software giant in the Cabal (The Conficker Working Group).

John Crain, ICANN Senior Director for Security, Stability, and Resiliency, the British-born point man for ICANN contribution to the Cabal, who secured cooperation from Top Level Domains worldwide. He lives in Long Beach, California.

Andre DiMino, a cofounder of Shadowserver.com, a nonprofit botnet-hunting service, was one of the first to sinkhole and study Conficker, from his home in New Jersey.

Rodney Joffe, South African–born head of security for Neustar, Inc. A successful entrepreneur now based in Phoenix, he holds several patents and is an internationally known expert in Internet security. He has been a White House adviser on cybersecurity issues and is the official head of the Cabal.

Chris Lee, Georgia Tech grad student who took over the Cabal's sinkholing operation. He now works for the Department of Homeland Security.

Andre "Dre" Ludwig, a North Virginia–based consultant, now a senior manager for Neustar, Inc., handling Top Level Domain security, who was responsible for technical strategy within the Cabal, technical verification, and was liaison to the security industry.

Ramses Martinez, Information Security Director of VeriSign, Inc., which operates two of the Internet's thirteen root servers from Dulles, Virginia.

Phil Porras, Program Director for SRI International in Menlo Park, California, was one of the first to study Conficker and spearheaded efforts to predict its behavior and defeat it. He led the Cabal's reverse engineering subgroup.

Hassen Saidi, a native of Algeria with a PhD in computer studies, who was the primary reverse engineer on Phil Porras's staff at SRI International. He dissected the various strains of Conficker as they appeared.

Paul Twomey, CEO and President of ICANN in Marina Del Rey, California, during the fight to contain Conficker.

Paul Vixie, an American Internet pioneer based in San Francisco, outspokenly critical of the way the Internet is structured and the flaws in the Windows Operating System. Founder, Chairman, and Chief Scientist for the Internet Systems Consortium.

Rick Wesson, CEO of Support Intelligence and owner of Alice's Registry, based in San Francisco, one of the founding (and most controversial) members of the Cabal, who initiated the strategy of containing Conficker by anticipating and buying up domain names generated by the worm's algorithm.

WORM

1

ZERO

NEW MUTANT ACTIVITY REGISTERED
—X-Men; The Age of Apocalypse

The new worm in Phil Porras's digital petri dish was announced in the usual way: a line of small black type against a white backdrop on one of his three computer screens, displaying just the barest of descriptors—time of arrival . . . server type . . . point of origin . . . nineteen columns in all.

The readout began:

```
17:52:00 . . . Win2K-f . . . 201.212.167.29
(NET.AR): PRIMA S.A, BUENOS AIRES,
BUENOS AIRES, AR. (DSL) . . .
```

It was near the end of the workday for most Californians, November 20, 2008, a cool evening in Menlo Park. Phil took no notice of the newcomer at first. Scores of these

1

digital infections were recorded on his monitor every day, each a simple line on his Daily Infections Log—actually, his "Multiperspective Malware Infection Analysis Page." This was the 137th that day. It had an Internet Protocol (IP) address from Argentina. Spread out across the screen were the infection's vitals, including one column that noted how familiar it was to the dozens of antivirus (AV) companies who ride herd on malicious software (malware). Most were instantly familiar. For instance, the one just above was known to all 33 of the applicable AV vendors. The one before that: 35 out of 36.

This one registered a zero in the recognition column: 0 of 37. This is what caught his eye when he first noticed it on his Log.

Zero.

Outside it was dark, but as usual Phil was still at his desk in a small second-story office on the grounds of SRI International, a busy hive of labs, hundreds of them, not far from Stanford University. It is a crowded cluster of very plain three-story tan-and-maroon buildings arrayed around small parking lots like rectangular building blocks. There is not a lot of green space. It is a node of condensed brainpower, one of the best-funded centers for applied science in the world, and with about seventeen hundred workers is the second-largest employer in Menlo Park. It began life as the Stanford Research Institute—hence the initials SRI—but it was spun off by the university forty years ago. It's a place where ideas become reality, the birthplace of gizmos like the computer mouse, ultrasound imagery machines, or tiny robot drones. The trappings of Phil's office are simple: a white leather couch, a lamp, and a desk, which is mostly taken up by his array of three computer monitors. On the walls are whiteboards filled with calculations and schematics and several framed photos of vintage World War II fighter planes, vestiges of a boyhood passion for model building. The view out his window, through a few leafy branches, is of an identical building across an enclosed yard. It could be any office in any industrial park in any state in America. But what's remarkable about the view from behind Phil's desk has nothing to do with what's outside his window. It's on those monitors. Spread out in his desktop array of glowing multicolored pixels is a vista of cyberspace equal to . . . say, the state of Texas.

One of the inventions SRI pioneered was the Internet. The research center is a cornerstone of the global phenomenon; it owned one of the first two computers formally linked together in 1969, the first strand of a web that today links billions. This was more than two decades before Al Gore popularized the term "information superhighway." There at the genesis, every computer that connected to the nascent network was assigned its own 32-bit identity number or IP address, represented in four octets of ones and zeros. Today the sheer size of the Internet has necessitated a new system that uses 128-bit addresses. SRI ceded authority for assigning and keeping track of such things years ago, but it retains ownership of a very large chunk of cyberspace. Phil's portion of it is a relatively modest, nothing-to-brag-about-but-damned-hard-to-get, "slash 16," a block of the original digital universe containing 65,536 unique IP addresses—in other words, the last two octets of its identity number are variable, so that there are two to the sixteenth (2^{16}) possible distinct addresses, one for each potential machine added to its network. It gives him what he calls "a large contact surface" on the Internet. He's like a rancher with his boots propped on the rail on the front porch before a wide-open prairie with, as the country song says, *miles of lonesome* in every direction. It's good for spotting intruders.

Phil's specialty is computer security, or, rather, Internet security, because few computers today are not linked to others. Each is part of a network tied to another larger network that is in turn linked to a still larger one, and so on, forming an intricate invisible web of electrons that today circle the Earth and reach even to the most distant parts of our galaxy (if you count those wayfaring NASA robot vehicles sending back cool snapshots from mankind's farthest reach into space). This web is the singular marvel of the modern age, a kind of global brain, the world at everyone's fingertips. It is a tool so revolutionary that we have just begun to glimpse its potential—for good and for evil.

Out on his virtual front porch, Phil keeps his eyes peeled for trouble. Most of what he sees is routine, the viral annoyances that have bedeviled computer users everywhere for decades, illustrating the principle that any new tool, no matter how helpful, will also be used for harm. Viruses are responsible for such things as the spamming of your in-box with come-ons for penis enlargement or million-dollar investment opportunities in Nigeria. Some malware is designed to damage or destroy your computer, or threaten to do so unless you purchase a remedy (which turns out to be fake). When you get hit, you know it. But the newest, most sophisticated computer viruses, like the most successful biological viruses, have bigger ambitions, and are designed for stealth. They would be noticed only by the most technically capable and vigilant of geeks. For these, you have to be looking.

Anything new was enough to make Phil's spine tingle. He had been working with computers since he was in high school in Whittier, California, and had sent away in 1984 for a build-it-yourself personal computer. Back then personal computers had begun to establish a wider market, but there were still small companies who catered to a fringe community of users, most of them teenagers, who were excited enough and smart enough to order kits and assemble the machines themselves, using them to play games, mostly, or configure them to perform simple household or business chores. Phil's dad was an accountant, and his mom ran a care center for senior citizens, so he amazed them by programming his toy to handle time-consuming, monotonous tasks. But mostly he played games. He took computer classes in high school, contributing at least as much as he took away, and in college at the University of California, Irvine, he fell in with a group of like-minded geeks who amused themselves by showing off their programming skills. At the time—this was in the late 1980s—Sun Microsystems dominated the software world with "Solaris," an operating system with a reputation for state-of-the-art security features. Phil and his friends engaged in a game of one-upmanship, hacking into the terminals in their college labs and playing pranks on each other. Some of the stunts were painful. Victims might lose a whole night of work because their opponent had remotely reprogrammed their keyboard to produce gibberish. So Phil's introduction to computer warfare, even at this prank stage, had real consequences. It was a world where you either understood the operating system enough to fend off an attack, or got screwed.

This kind of competition—mind you, these were very few geeks competing for very small stakes—nevertheless turned Phil into an aggressive expert in computer security. So much so that when he graduated, he had to go shopping for a professor at the graduate level who could teach him something. He found one in Richard Kemmerer at the University of California at Santa Barbara (UCSB), one of the only computer security academics in the country at the time, who quickly recognized Phil as more of a peer than a student. The way you capitalized on superior hacking skills in academia was to anticipate invasion strategies and devise way of detecting and fending them off. Phil was soon recognized as an expert in the newly emerging field. Today, UCSB has one of the most advanced computer security departments in the world, but back in the early 1990s, Phil was it. When UNIX-5 was purported to be the most secure operating system in the business, Phil cooked up fifty ways to break into it. When he was twenty years old, he was invited to a convention on computer security at SRI, where he presented his first attempts to design software that would auto-detect his impressive array of exploits. The research institute snapped him up when he finished his degree, and over the next two decades Phil's expertise has evolved with the industry.

Phil has seen malware grow from petty vandalism to major crime. Today it is often crafted by organized crime syndicates or, more recently, by nation-states. An effusive man with light brown skin and a face growing rounder as he approaches middle age, he wears thin-framed glasses that seem large for his face, and has thick brown hair that jumps straight up on top. Phil is a nice guy, a *good guy*. One might even say he's a kind of superhero. In cyberspace, there really are bad guys and good guys locked in intense cerebral combat; one side cruises the Internet for pillage and plunder, the other to prevent it. In this struggle, Phil is nothing less than a giant in the army of all that is right and true. His work is filled with urgent purpose and terrific challenges, a high-stakes game of one-upmanship in a realm that few people comprehend. Like most people who love their work, Phil enjoys talking about it, to connect, to explain—but the effort is often doomed:

. . . *So what we ended up doing is, see, we ended up becoming really good at getting ourselves infected. Like through a sandnet. Executing the malware. Finding the IRC site and channel that was being exploited by the botmaster and simply going after it. Talking to the ISP and directly attacking. Bringing it down. Bringing down the IRC server or redirecting all IRC communications to use* . . .

He tries hard. He speaks in clipped phrases, ratcheting down his natural mental velocity. But still the sentences come fast. Crisp. To the point. You can hear him straining to avoid the tricky territory of broader context, but then, failing, inevitably, as his unstoppable enthusiasm for the subject matter slips out of low gear and he's off at turbo speed into Wired World: . . . *bringing down the IRC server* . . . *the current UTC date* . . . *exploiting the buffer's capacity* . . . *utilizing the peer-to-peer mechanism* . . . Suffice it to say, Phil is a man who has come face-to-face many times with the Glaze, the unmistakable look of profound confusion and uninterest that descends whenever a conversation turns to the inner workings of a computer.

The Glaze is familiar to every geek ever called upon to repair a malfunctioning machine—*Look, dude, spare me the details, just fix it!* Most people, even well-educated people with formidable language skills, folks with more than a passing knowledge of word-processing software and spreadsheets and dynamic graphical displays, people who spend hours every day with their fingertips on keyboards, whose livelihoods and even leisure-time preferences increasingly depend on fluency with a variety of software, remain utterly clueless about how any of it works. The innards of mainframes and operating systems and networks are considered not just unfathomable but somehow unknowable, or even *not worth knowing*, in the way that many people are content to regard electricity as voodoo. The technical side of the modern world took a sharp turn with the discovery of electricity, and then accelerated off the ramp with electromagnetism into the Realm of the Hopelessly Obtuse, so that everyday life has come to coexist in strict parallel with a mysterious techno dimension. Computer technology rubs shoulders with us every day, as real as can be, even vital, only . . . also . . . *not real.* Virtual. Transmitting signals through thin air. Grounded in machines with no visible moving parts. This techno dimension is alive with . . . what exactly? Well-ordered trains of electrons? Binary charges?

That digital ranch Phil surveys? It doesn't actually exist, of course, at least not in the sense of dust and sand and mesquite trees and whirling buzzards and distant blue buttes. It exists only in terms of capacity, or potential.

Concepts like bits and bytes, domain names, ISPs, IPAs, RPCs, P2P protocols, infinite loops, and cloud computing are strictly the province of geeks or nerds who bother to pay attention to such things, and who are, ominously, increasingly essential in some obscure and vaguely disturbing way to the smooth functioning of civilization. They remain, by definition, so far as the stereotype goes, odd, remote, reputed to be borderline autistic, and generally opaque to anyone outside their own tribe—THEY ARE MUTANTS, BORN WITH ABILITIES FAR BEYOND THOSE OF NORMAL HUMANS. The late M.I.T. professor Joseph Weizenbaum identified and described the species back at the dawn of the digital age, in his 1976 book *Computer Power and Human Reason*:

> Wherever computer centers have become established, that is to say, in countless places in the United States, as well as in all other industrial regions of the world, bright young men of disheveled appearance, often with sunken glowing eyes, can be seen sitting at their computer consoles, their arms tensed and waiting to fire their fingers, already poised to strike, at the buttons and keys on which their attention seems to be riveted as a gambler's on the rolling dice. When not so transfixed, they often sit at tables strewn with computer printouts over which they pore like possessed students of a cabalistic text. They work until they nearly drop, twenty, thirty hours at a time. Their food, if they arrange it, is brought to them: Cokes, sandwiches. If possible, they sleep on

cots near the computer. But only for a few hours—then back to the console or printouts. Their rumpled clothes, their unwashed and unshaven faces, and their uncombed hair all testify that they are oblivious to their bodies and the world in which they move. They exist, at least when so engaged, only through and for computers. These are computer bums, compulsive programmers. They are an international phenomenon.

The Geek Tribe today has broadened to include a wider and more wholesome variety of characters—Phil played a lot of basketball in high school and actually went out with girls—and there is no longer any need need for "printouts" to obsess over—everything is on-screen—but the Tribe remains international and utterly obsessed, linked 24/7 by email and a host of dedicated Internet chat channels. In one sense, it is strictly egalitarian. You might be a lonely teenager with pimples in some suburban basement, too smart for high school, or the CEO of some dazzling Silicon Valley start-up, but you can join the Tribe so long as you know your stuff. Nevertheless, its upper echelons remain strictly elitist; they can be as snobby as the hippest Soho nightclub. Some kind of sniff test applies. Phil himself, for instance, was kept out of the inner circle of geeks fighting this new worm for about a month, even though he and his team at SRI had been at it well before the Cabal came together, and much of the entire effort rested on their work. Access to a mondo mainframe or funding source might gain you some cachet, but real traction comes only with savvy and brainpower. In a way, the Tribe is as virtual as the cyberworld itself. Many members have known each other for years without actually having ever met in, like, *real life*. Phil seems happiest here, in the glow of his three monitors, plugged into his elite global confederacy of the like-minded.

The world they inhabit didn't even exist, in any form, when Phil was born in 1966. At that point the idea of linking computers together was just that, an idea, and a half-baked one. It was the brainchild of a group of forward-thinking scientists at the Pentagon's Advanced Research Projects Agency (ARPA). The agency was housed in and funded by the Pentagon, and this fact has led to false stories about the Internet's origins, that it was *official* and *military* and therefore inherently nefarious. But ARPA was one of the least military enterprises in the building. Indeed, the agency was created and sustained as a way of keeping basic civilian research alive in an institution otherwise entirely focused on war. One of the things ARPA did was underwrite basic science at universities, supporting civilian academic scientists in projects often far afield from any obvious military application. Since at that time the large laboratories were using computers more and more, one consequence of coordinating ARPA's varied projects was that it accumulated a variety of computer terminals in its Pentagon offices, each wired to mainframes at the different labs. Every one of these terminals was different. They varied in appearance and function, because each was a remote arm of the hardware and software peculiar to its host mainframe. Each had its own method of transferring and displaying data. ARPA's Pentagon office had begun to resemble the tower of Babel.

Computers were then so large that if you bought one, you needed a loading dock to receive it, or you needed to lift off the roof and lower it into position with a crane. Each machine had its own design and its own language and, once it had been put to work in a particular lab, its own culture, because each was programmed and managed to perform certain functions peculiar to the organization that bought it. Most computers were used to crunch numbers for military or scientific purposes. As with many new inventions that have vast potential, those who first used them didn't look far past their own immediate needs, which were demanding and remarkable enough, like calculating the arc through the upper atmosphere of a newly launched missile, or working out the variable paths of subatomic particles in a physics experiment. Computers were very good at solving large, otherwise time-consuming calculations very quickly, thus enabling all kinds of amazing technological feats, not the least of which was to steer six teams of astronauts to the surface of the moon and back.

Most thinkers were busy with all of the immediate miracles computers had made suddenly doable; only those at the farthest speculative frontiers were pondering the machines' broader possibilities. The scientists at ARPA, J. C. R. Licklider and Bob Taylor and Larry Roberts, as described in *Where Wizards Stay Up Late,* by Katie Hafner and Matthew Lyon, were convinced that the computer might someday be the ultimate aid to human intelligence, that it might someday be, in a sense, perched on mankind's shoulder making instant connections that few would have the knowledge, experience, or recall to make on their own, connecting minds around the world in real time, providing instant analysis of concepts that in the past might require years of painstaking research. The first idea was just to share data between labs, but it was only a short leap from sharing data to sharing *resources*: in other words, enabling a researcher at one lab to tap into the special capabilities and libraries of a computer at a distant one. Why reinvent a program on your own mainframe when it was already up and running elsewhere? The necessary first step in this direction would be linkage. A way had to be found to knit the independent islands of computers at universities and research centers into a functional whole.

There was resistance. Some of those operating mainframes, feeling privileged and proprietary and comfortably self-contained, saw little or no advantage in sharing them. For one thing, competition for computing time in the big labs was already keen. Why invite more competition from remote locations? Since each mainframe spoke its own language, and many were made by competing companies, how much time and effort and precious computing power would it take to enable smooth communication? The first major conceptual breakthrough was the idea of building separate computers just to resolve these issues. Called Interface Message Processors (IMPs), they grew out of an idea floated by Washington University professor Wesley Clark in 1967: instead of asking each computer operator to design protocols for sending and receiving data to every other computer on the net, why not build a subnet just to manage the traffic? That way each host computer would need to learn only one language, that of the IMP. And the IMPs would manage the routing and translating problems. This idea even dangled before each lab the prospect of a new mainframe to play with *at no extra cost*, since the government was footing the bill. It turned an imposition into a gift. By the early 1970s, there were dozens of IMPs scattered around the country, a subnet, if you will, managing traffic on the ARPANET. As it happens, the first two computers linked in this way were a Scientific Data Systems (SDS) 940 model in Menlo Park, and an older model, SDS Sigma-7, at UCLA. That was in October 1969. Phil Porras was just out of diapers.

The ARPANET's designers had imagined resource- and data-sharing as its primary purpose, and a greatly simplified way to coordinate the agency's scattered projects, but as the authors of new life-forms have always discovered, from God Almighty to Dr. Frankenstein, the creature immediately had ideas of its own. From its earliest days, the Internet was more than the sum of its parts. The first hugely successful unforeseen application became email, the ability to send messages instantly anywhere in the world, followed closely by message lists, or forums that linked in real time those with a shared interest, no matter where they were. Message lists or chat lines were created for disciplines serious and not so serious—the medieval game "Dungeons and Dragons" was a popular early topic. By the mid-1970s, at about the time microcomputers were first being marketed as build-it-yourself kits (attracting the attention of Harvard undergrad nerds Bill Gates and Paul Allen), the ARPANET had created something new and unforeseen: in the words of Hafner and Lyon, "a community of equals, many of whom had never met each other yet who carried on as if they had known each other all of their lives . . . perhaps the first virtual community."

This precursor web relied on telephone lines to carry information, but in short order computers were being linked by radio (the ALOHANET in Hawaii connected computers on four islands in this way) and increasingly by satellite (the quickest way to connect computers on different continents). Pulling together this rapidly growing variety of networks meant going back to the idea of the IMP: creating a new subnet to facilitate linkage—call it a sub-subnet, or a network of networks. Computer scientists Vint Cerf of Stanford and Bob Kahn of MIT presented a paper in 1974 outlining a new method for moving data between these disparate systems, called Transmission Control Protocol, or TCP. It was another eureka moment. It enabled any computer network established anywhere in the world to plug into the growing international system, no matter how it transmitted data.

All of this was happening years before most people had ever seen an actual computer. For its first twenty years, the Internet remained the exclusive preserve of computer scientists and experts at military and intelligence centers, but it was becoming increasingly clear to them that the tool had broader application. Today it serves more than two billion users around the world, and has increasingly become the technological backbone of modern life.

Its growth has been bottom-up, in that beyond ad hoc efforts to shape its technical undergirding, no central authority has dictated its structure or imposed rules or guidelines for its use. This has generated a great deal of excitement among social theorists. The assignment of domain names and IP Addresses was handed off by SRI in 1998 to the closest thing the Internet has to a governing body, the International Corporation for Assigned Names and Numbers (ICANN). Headquartered in Marina Del Rey, California, ICANN is strictly nonprofit and serves little more than a clerical role, but, as we shall see, is capable of exerting important moral authority in a crisis. Domain names are the names (sometimes just numbers) that a user

selects to represent his presence on the Internet—yahoo.
com; nytimes.com, etc.. Many domains also establish a
website, a "page" or visible representation of the domain's
owner, be it an individual, a corporation, an agency, an
institution, or whatever. Not all domains establish websites.
The physical architecture of the Internet rests on thirteen
root servers, labeled A, B, C . . . through M. Ten of these
are in the United States, and one each in Great Britain,
Japan, and Sweden.* The root servers maintain very large
computers to direct the constant flow of data worldwide.

*This is a simplification, and is not exactly true, in the sense of there being
physically thirteen servers at those locations acting as central switchboards
for the Internet. Like all things in cyberspace . . . it's complicated. Here's
how Paul Vixie attempted to explain it to me: "There are thirteen root
name servers on which all traffic on the Internet depends, but what we're
talking about are root name server identities, not actual machines. Each
one has a name, like mine, which is f.root-servers.net. A few of them are
actual servers. Most of them are virtual servers, mirrored or replicated
in dozens of places. Each root server is vital, sort of, to every, sort of,
message, sort of. They are vital (but not necessarily involved) in every
TCP/IP [Transmission Control Protocol/Internet Protocol] connection,
since every TCP/IP connection depends on DNS [Domain Name System],
and DNS depends on the root name servers. But the root name servers are
not in the data path itself. They do not carry other people's traffic, they
just answer questions. The most frequent question we hear is, 'What is the
TCP/IP address for www.google.com?' and the most frequent answer we
give is 'I dunno but I will tell you where the COM. Servers are and you
can ask them.' Once a TCP/IP connection is set up, DNS is no longer
involved. If a browser or email system makes a second or subsequent
connection to the same place in a short time, it'll have the TCP/IP address
saved in a cache, and DNS won't be involved. A root name server is an
Internet resource having a particular name and address. But it's possible
to offer the same resource at the same name and address from multiple
locations. f.root-servers.net, which is my root name server, is located in
fifty or so cities around the globe, each independent of the others but all
sharing an identity." Got that?

The root servers also maintain comprehensive and dynamic lists of domain-name servers, which keep the flow moving in the right direction, from nanosecond to nanosecond.

The system works more like an organism than any traditional notion of a machine. The best effort at a visual illustration was created by researchers at Bar-Ilan University in Israel, who produced a gorgeous image that resembles nothing so much as a *single cell*. It shows a dense glowing orange nucleus of eighty or so central nodes surrounded by a diffuse protoplasmic periphery of widely scattered yellow-and-green specks representing isolated smaller nodes, encircled by a dense blue- and-purple outer wall or membrane of directly linked, peer-to-peer networks. The bright hot colors indicate high-traffic links, like root servers or large academic, government, or corporate networks; the cooler blues and purples of the outer membrane suggest the low-traffic networks of local Internet Service Providers (ISPs) or companies. There is something deeply suggestive in this map, reminiscent of what Douglas Hofstadter called a "strange loop" in his classic work, *Gödel, Escher, Bach,* the notion that a complex system tends toward self-reference, and inevitably rises toward consciousness. It is possible, gazing at this remarkable picture of the working Internet, to imagine it growing, multiplying, diversifying, and some day, in some epochal instant, blinking and turning and looking up, becoming *alive*. Planetary consciousness. The *global I*.

The Internet is not about to wink at us just yet, but it

helps explain some of the reverence felt by those engaged in conceptualizing, building, and maintaining the thing. It represents something entirely new in human history, and is the single most remarkable technological achievement of our age. Scientists discovered the great advantage of sharing lab results and ideas instantaneously with others in their field all over the world, and grew excited about the possibilities of tying large networks together to perform unprecedented research. Social theorists awoke to the thing's potential, and a new vision of a techno utopia was born. All human knowledge at everyone's fingertips! Ideas shared, critiqued, tested, and improved! Events in the most remote corners of the world experienced everywhere simultaneously! The web would be a repository for all human knowledge, a global marketplace for products and ideas, a forum for anything that required interaction, from delicate international diplomacy to working out complex differential equations to buying office supplies— and it would be entirely free of regulation and control! Governments would be powerless to censor information. Journalism and publishing and research would no longer be in the hands of a wealthy few. Secrets would be impossible to keep! The Internet promised a truly global egalitarian age. That was the idea, anyway. The international and unstructured nature of the thing was vital to these early Internet idealists. If knowledge is power, then power at long last would reside where it belonged, with the people, *all people!* Tyrants and oligarchs would tremble! Bureaucracy would be streamlined! Barriers between nation-states and cultures would crumble! *Humankind would at last be . . . !*

. . . you get the picture.

Some of this was undeniable. Few innovations have taken root so fast internationally, and few have evolved in such an unfettered, democratic way. The Internet has made everyone, in a virtual sense, a citizen of the world, a development that has already had profound consequences for millions, and is sure to have more. But in their early excitement, the architects of the Internet may have overvalued its anarchic essence. When the civilian Internet began taking shape, mostly connecting university labs to one another, the only users were people who understood computers and computer languages. *Techno-utopia!* Everyone can play! Information for free! Complete transparency! No one wrote rules for the net; instead, people floated "Requests for Comment." Ideas for keeping the thing working smoothly were kicked around by everyone until a consensus arose, and given the extreme flexibility of software, anything adopted could readily be changed. Nobody was actually in charge. This openness and lack of any centralized control is both a strength and a weakness. If no one is ultimately responsible for the Internet, then how do you police and defend it? Unless everyone using the thing is well-intentioned, it is vulnerable to attack, and can be used as easily for harm as for good.

Even though it has become a part of daily life, the Internet itself remains a cloudy idea to most people. It's nebulous in a deeper way than previous leaps in home technology. Take the radio. Nobody knew how that worked, but you could picture invisible waves of electromagnetic particles arriving from the distance like the surf, distant voices carried forth on waves from the edges of the earth and amplified for your ears. If you lived in a valley or the shadow of a big building, the mountains or the walls got in the way of the waves; if you lived too far from the source of the signal, then the waves just petered out. You got static, or no sound. A fellow could understand that much. Or TV . . . well, nobody understood that, except that it was like the damn radio only the waves, the invisible waves, were more *complex,* see, and hence delivered pictures, too, and the sorting mechanism in the box, the transistors or vacuum tubes or some such, projected those pictures inside the tube. In either case you needed antennae to pick up the waves and vibrate just so. There was something going on there you could picture, even if falsely. But the Internet is just there. It is all around us, like the old idea of luminiferous ether. No antenna. No waves—at least, none of the kind readily understood. And it contains not just a voice or picture, but . . . the *whole world and everything in it*: pictures, sounds, text, movies, maps, art, propaganda, music, news, games, mail, whole national libraries, books, magazines, newspapers, sex (in varieties from enticing to ghastly), along with close-up pictures of

Mars and Jupiter, your long-forgotten great-aunt Margaret, the menu at your local Thai restaurant, everything you ever heard of and plenty you had not ever dreamed about, all of it just waiting to be plucked out of thin air.

Behind his array of three monitors in Menlo Park, Phil Porras occupies a desk in the very birthplace of this marvel, and sees it not in some vague sense, but as something very real, comprehensible, and alarmingly fragile. By design, a portion of the virtual ranch he surveys is left unfenced and undefended. It is thus an inviting target for every free-roaming strain of malware trolling cyberspace. This is his petri dish, or honeynet. Inside the very large computer he gets to play with, Porras creates a network of "virtual computers." These are not physical machines, just individual operating systems within the large computer that mimic the functions of distinct, small ones. Each has its own IP address. So Phil can set up the equivalent of a computer network that exists entirely within the confines of his digital ranch. These days if you leave any computer linked to the Internet unprotected, you can just sit back and watch it "get popped" or "get pwned," in the parlance. (The unpronounceable coinage "pwned" was an example of puckish hacker humor: geeks are notoriously bad spellers, and someone early on in the malware wars had typed "p" instead of "o" in typing out the word "owned." It stuck.) If you own an Internet space as wide as SRI's, you can watch your virtual computers get *pwned* every few minutes.

Like just about everything in this field, the nomenclature for computer infections is confusing, because normal folk tend to use the terms "virus" and "worm" interchangeably, while the Tribe defines them differently. To make matters worse, the various species in the growing taxonomy sometimes cross-pollinate. The overarching term "malware" refers to any program that infects a computer and operates without the user's consent. For the purposes of this story, the difference between a "virus" and a "worm" is in the way each spreads. To invade a computer, a virus relies on human help such as clicking unadvisedly on an unsolicited email attachment, or inserting an infected floppy disk or thumb drive into a vulnerable computer. A worm, on the other hand, is state of the art. It can spread all by itself.

The new arrival in Phil's honeypot was clearly a worm, and it began to attract the Tribe's attention immediately. After that first infection at 5:20 p.m. Thursday there came a few classic bits of malware, and then the newcomer again. And then again. And again. The infection rate kept accelerating. By Friday morning, Phil's colleague Vinod Yegneswaran notified him that their honeynet was under significant attack. By then, very little else was showing on the Infections Log. The worm was spreading exponentially, crowding in so fast that it shouldered aside all the ordinary daily fare. If the typical inflow of infection was like a steady drip from a faucet, this new strain seemed shot out of a fire hose.

Its most obvious characteristics were familiar at a glance.

The worm was targeting—Phil could see this on his Log—Port 445 of the Windows Operating System, the most commonly used operating software in the world, causing a buffer at that port to overflow, then corrupting its execution in order to burrow into the host computer's memory. Whatever this strain was, it was the most contagious he had ever seen. It turned each new machine it infected into a propagation demon, rapidly scanning for new targets, reaching out voraciously. Soon he began to hear from others in the Tribe, who were seeing the same thing. They were watching it flood in from Germany, Japan, Colombia, Argentina, and various points around the United States. It was a pandemic.

Months later, when the battle over this worm was fully joined, Phil would check with his friends at the University of California, San Diego (UCSD), who operate a supercomputer that owns a "darknet," or a "black hole," a continent-size portion of cyberspace. Theirs is a "slash eight," which amounts to one 256th of the entire Internet. Any random scanning worm like this new one would land in UCSD's black hole once every 256 times it launched from a new source. When they went looking, they found that the first Conficker scan attempt had hit them three minutes before the worm first hit Phil's honeynet. The source for their infection would turn out to be the same— the IP address in Buenos Aires. The address itself didn't mean much. Most Internet Service Providers reassigned an

IP address each time a machine connects to the network. But behind that number on that day had been the original worm, possibly its author but more likely a drone computer under his control.

The honeynets at SRI and at UCSD were designed to snare malware in order to study it. But the worm wasn't just cascading into their networks. This was a worldwide digital blitzkrieg. Existing firewalls and antiviral software didn't recognize it, so they weren't slowing it down. The next questions were: Why? What was it up to? What was the worm's purpose?

The most likely initial guess was that it was building a botnet. Not all worms assemble botnets, but they are very good at doing so. This would explain the extraordinary propagation rate. The term "bot" is short for "robot." Various kinds of malware turn computers into slaves controlled by an illicit, outside operator. Programmers, who as a class share a weakness for sci-fi and horror films, also call them zombies. In the case of this new worm, the robot analogy is more apt.

Imagine your computer as a big spaceship, like the starship *Enterprise* on *Star Trek*. The ship is so complex and sophisticated that even an experienced commander like Captain James T. Kirk has only a general sense of how every facet of it works. From his wide swivel chair on the bridge, he can order it to fly, maneuver, and fight, but he cannot fully control or even comprehend all its inner workings. The ship contains many complex, interrelated systems, each with its own function and history—systems for, say, guidance, maneuvers, power, air and water, communications, temperature control, weapons, defensive measures, etc. Each system has its own operator, performing routine maintenance, exchanging information, making fine adjustments, keeping it running or ready. When idling or cruising, the ship essentially runs itself without a word from Captain Kirk. It obeys when he issues a command, and then returns to its latent mode, busily doing its own thing until the next time it is needed.

Now imagine a clever invader, an enemy infiltrator, who *does* understand the inner workings of the ship. He knows it well enough to find a portal with a broken lock overlooked by the ship's otherwise vigilant defenses—like, say, a flaw in Microsoft's operating platform. So no one notices when he slips in. He trips no alarm, and then, to prevent another clever invader from exploiting the same weakness, he repairs the broken lock and seals the portal shut behind him. He *improves* the ship's defenses. Ensconced securely inside, he silently sets himself up as the ship's alternate commander. The *Enterprise* is now a "bot." The invader enlists the various operating functions of the ship to do his bidding, careful to avoid tripping any alarms. Captain Kirk is still up on the bridge in his swivel chair with the magnificent instrument arrays, unaware that he now has a rival in the depths of his ship. The *Enterprise* continues to perform as it always did. Meanwhile, the invader begins surreptitiously communicating with his own distant commander, letting him know that he is in position and ready, waiting for instructions.

And now imagine a vast fleet, in which the *Enterprise* is only one ship among millions, all of them infiltrated in exactly the same way, each ship with its hidden pilot, ever alert to an outside command. In the real world, this infiltrated fleet is called a "botnet," a network of infected, "robot" computers. The first job of a botnet-assembling worm is to infect and link together as many computers as possible. Thousands of botnets exist, most of them relatively small—a few tens of thousand or a few hundreds of thousands of infected computers. More than a billion computers are in use around the world, and by some estimates, a fourth of them have been joined to a botnet.

Most of us still think of the threat posed by malware in terms of what it might do to our personal computer. When the subject comes up, the questions are: How do I know if I'm infected? How do I get rid of the infection? But modern malware is aimed less at exploiting individual computers than exploiting the Internet. A botnet-creating worm doesn't want to harm your computer; it wants to *use* it.

Botnets are exceedingly valuable tools for criminal enterprise. Among other things, they can be used to efficiently distribute malware, to steal private information from otherwise secure websites or computers, to assist in fraudulent schemes, or to launch Dedicated Denial of Service (DDoS) attacks—overwhelming a targeted server with a flood of requests for response. If you control even a minor botnet, one with, say, twenty thousand computers, you own enough computing power to shut down most business networks. The creator of an effective botnet, one with a wide range and the staying power to defeat security measures, can use it himself for one of the above scams, or he can sell or lease it to people who will. Botnets are traded in underground markets online. Customers shop for specific things, like, say, fifty computers that belong to the FBI, or a thousand computers that are owned by Google, or Bank of America, or the U.S. or British military. The cumulative power of a botnet has been used to extort protection money from large business networks, which will sometimes pay to avoid a crippling DDoS attack. Botnets can also be used to launder money. Opportunity for larceny and sabotage is limited only by the imagination and skill of the botmaster.

If the right orders were given, and all bots in a large net worked together in one concerted effort, they could crack most codes, break into and plunder just about any protected database in the world, and potentially hobble or even destroy almost any computer network, including networks that make up a country's vital modern infrastructure: systems that control banking, telephones, energy flow, air traffic, health-care information—even the Internet itself. Because the idea of the Internet is so nebulous, it is hard for most people, even in positions of public responsibility, to imagine it under attack, or destroyed. Those who specialize in cybersecurity face a wall of incomprehension and disbelief when they sound an alarm. It is as if this dangerous weapon pointed at the vitals of the digital world is something only they can see. And in recent years they face a new problem . . . *amusement.* The alarm has been sounded falsely too often—take the widespread fear of an international computer meltdown at the turn of the millennium, the Y2K phenomenon, which did not happen. This has conditioned the popular press to regard warnings from the Tribe in the same way it regards periodic predictions of the apocalypse from wacky televangelists. The news tends to be reported with a knowing wink, as if to say: And here's your latest prediction of divine wrath and global destruction from the guys who wear those funny plastic protectors in their shirt pockets. *Take it as seriously as you wish.* Oddly, as the de facto threat posed by malware grew, it became harder and harder to get people, even people in responsible positions, to take it seriously.

If yours is one of the infected machines, you are like Captain Kirk, seemingly in full command of your ship, unaware that you have a hidden rival, or that your computer is part of this vast robot fleet. The worm inside your machine is not idle. It is stealthily running, scanning for other computers to infect, issuing small maintenance commands, working to protect itself from being discovered and removed, biding its time, and periodically checking in with its command center. The threat posed by a botnet is less to individual computer owners than to society at large. The Internet today is in its Wild West stage. You link to it at your own risk.

Phil had no way to stop the spread of this new worm. He could only study it. And he could tell little about it at first. He knew roughly where his first sample had come from, and that it was something unrecognized. He knew that it was a genius of a propagator. It had one other curious feature that he had never seen. It had a geographic look-up capability: this worm wanted to know where the machine it had just infected was located in the real world.

The first step in dealing with any new malware is to "unpack" it, to break it open and look inside. Most malware comes in a protective shell of code, complex enough to keep amateurs from taking a close look, but Phil's Menlo Park wizards were pros. They had invented an unpacking program they called Eureka that readily cracked open 95 percent of what they saw.

When they tried it on the new worm, it failed.

Sometimes when Phil was stymied like this, he would just wait for one of the AV vendors to meet the challenge. But this worm was flooding in so fast that waiting was not an option. His Infections Log showed the same thing over and over again, as the worm flooded in from everywhere.

As he would later explain, "There was literally nothing else for us to do."

2

MS08-067

The first reports of the new worm came to T. J. Campana from everywhere: in the form of instant messages and emails; from Phil Porras at SRI; from experts at Symantec, which markets the Norton AntiVirus software; from the network security geeks at iDefense; from F-Secure, a Finnish security firm; and from many others. This was on the first night.

"Hey, we're seeing something really weird."

"Something's happening."

T.J. wasn't surprised. He knew what it was. He had been waiting for a worm like this one for months.

He is program manager for security at Microsoft's Digital

Crimes Unit, which is to say that he is engaged in ceaseless warfare. Since Windows is the primary operating system for computers worldwide, it is the primary target for those seeking to infiltrate, destroy, pilfer, or hijack computers for nefarious purposes. In addition to developing and marketing its operating system and software, the company is increasingly engaged in this running battle. It's a very sophisticated contest. Malware is a thriving global industry, fleecing Microsoft's customers with scams that range from the crude and obvious, sexual come-ons and mountebank schemes, to the more subtle, like this worm, which was rapidly and silently assembling what threatened to become a very large botnet. T.J. is in charge of disrupting these constant incursions, and helping to catch those responsible. He and his colleagues labor to be proactive. They try to spot and patch vulnerabilities before the bad guys can fully exploit them—which is precisely what they had done with this one.

Microsoft's Redmond campus is a new and impressive corporate center outside Seattle that, at least from above, resembles . . . not a microchip exactly, although that would have been perfect, but the innards of an old watch. A spring-driven watch, with all its intricate gears, wheels, and escapement arms—albeit one with trees, sculptured lawns, and gardens. Viewed from above it contains a number of identical four-armed office buildings that curve toward rounded points at the end of each arm, like the teeth of simple sprockets. From the ground the giant sprockets are uniform in color, tan stone with green-tinted windows, and three stories high. There is an Erector Set feel to the place, a very tidy world where form rigorously follows function, where thousands of casually dressed young people in sneakers and jeans and wearing rumpled backpacks move under sheltered sidewalks like electrons marching along programmed routes, all of them fiercely pretending, in that laid-back Pacific Northwest way, not to be at work. Here is the home of the Windows Operating System, the software that mediates the computer experience for most of the billions of clueless who handle a keyboard or mouse every day. The sophisticated graphics-based wizardry of today's Windows rests on a fulcrum of the old MS-DOS system written in the 1970s, when Bill Gates and others got the immeasurably lucrative idea that computers should be easy to use even for those who knew nothing about how they worked, perhaps the premier jackpot notion of the twentieth century.

Gates and Paul Allen, his buddy from Lakeside, an exclusive Seattle prep school, had hit upon the idea of writing an easy-to-use computer operating system in 1974, after Allen saw a cover story in *Popular Electronics* about something entirely new, a personal computer. At a time of enormous, bulky mainframes, the Altair 8080 was a kit, marketed by a company called Micro Instrumentation and Telemetry Systems (MITS), that could be assembled into a working microcomputer in your own home. Few expected much of a market for it beyond avid computer hobbyists. If users managed to put it together correctly (many did not), they could operate it only by manipulating toggle switches to program the computer with object code, the ones and zeros of binary language. Gates and Allen were solidly in the demographic of the Altair 8080. They had fallen in love with computers at Lakeside as teenagers, and saw immediately that demand for the Altair would grow significantly if the machine were easier to use. They tailored a program to interpret BASIC, one of the earliest computer languages, and then sold it to MITS in Albuquerque in 1975. They incorporated as "Micro-Soft" at the same time, and launched the business that would make both young men superrich, along with a fair number of techies they enlisted to help them.

From the beginning, the genius of Microsoft had depended not only on technology but just as much—maybe even more—on shrewd business sense and careful market positioning, which seemed to come naturally to Gates in particular. The most lucrative step in the company's development came five years after the Altair, when IBM selected Microsoft (by then it had lost the hyphen) to provide the software for its entry into the burgeoning personal computer market. This was Microsoft-Disc Operating System (MS-DOS). IBM was the leading name in computers at the time. The computer giant had either been caught napping or deliberately waited out the early years of personal computer development (accounts vary), before introducing a home model designed to appeal to mainstream users, a machine that relied less on innovation than on standardization. Projecting that within the decade computers would be as commonplace in the home as TV sets, IBM intended to launch a microcomputer that borrowed the most successful features of the experimental machines being sold by Apple, Tandy, MITS, and other pioneers, and use its own manufacturing and promotional clout to grab the largest share of this emerging market. The product was a machine that could reliably and simply perform the most common tasks users asked of it—mostly word processing and simple statistical analysis. It had to be readily compatible with the large variety of software being written to capitalize on the home computing phenomenon. Gates and Allen had already proved themselves masters of this new art, and won the competition to handle the software side of the PC. When it proved successful beyond anyone's expectations, they rode its sales straight into the stratosphere.

Some of the world's youngest billionaires were minted. A generation of hopeful geeks began migrating to Silicon Valley with plans to conjure the next digital miracle. Perhaps the most remarkable thing about Microsoft was that its biggest coup was yet to come. It reached historic peaks of commercial fortune in a series of increasingly bold leaps.

After getting established with an operating system for the Altair 8080, and then scoring big with MS-DOS, Gates (Allen had by now withdrawn with his billions from an active role in the company) spurred his already large and extremely successful enterprise to create Windows, the most successful software venture ever. If we look back at MS-DOS today, it seems almost comically primitive and awkward. Home users were still working with a display screen that consisted of blinking lines of type on a dark screen, little more than the video equivalent of a typewriter display. Meanwhile, a host of exciting new applications were being developed that utilized the machine's mounting capabilities, most notably the ability to generate interactive visual images. The two primary ideas behind Windows were not new; they were known to the entire software industry in the 1980s. One was to design a Graphical User Interface (GUI) that would greatly simplify computer use by enabling users to point and click on visual images, or icons, instead of typing out commands. The second was to sandwich in a new layer of software, an Interface Manager, between the operating system and the applications—word processing, calculation, games, journalism, spreadsheet analysis, etc.— that would enable users to switch easily from one to the other, or even display multiple functions simultaneously. It would take Microsoft the rest of the decade to perfect Windows, even as Steve Jobs at Apple introduced Lisa and then the Macintosh 128K, which beat it to the market by a wide margin. Microsoft introduced two early versions of Windows in the 1980s that were widely considered inferior to the competition, but successfully overleaped everyone else in May 1990 with Windows 3.0. To accomplish it, Gates had hired experienced software developers away from competing firms, locked up agreements with more than twenty computer manufacturers to endorse the new system while it was still in development, and then strolled out on a stage in New York City to announce the breakthrough product in what he called "the most extravagant, extensive, and expensive [$3 million] software introduction ever." The awkward teenager, whose parents once forbade him to use a computer for months for fear his personal growth was being stunted by the machine, had evolved into not just a software innovator and skillful high-stakes businessman, but a showman. Windows took off immediately and just kept on selling. Gates became the richest man in the world, a pinnacle he owned for most of the next twenty years.

From the beginning, the software business was a cutthroat enterprise. Both hardware and software were relatively easy to clone and copy, so success from the earliest days meant both artfully borrowing from the competition and ferociously policing the borders of your own products. The first Windows operating system, introduced in 1985, was influenced by (critics have said "stolen from") ideas pioneered by other innovators. Gates became famous for his sharp elbows; to protect and enlarge Microsoft's franchise and his fortune, he took steps that some considered unfair and monopolistic—including the U.S. Department of Justice and the European Commission. Much of the disdain for Microsoft among members of the Geek Tribe stems from this fact. The software giant's riches and competitive excesses would probably be forgiven if Windows were seen as not just as the richest, but the best. Fairly or not, the opposite is the case. Many geeks view Windows' various great leaps forward—Windows 95, XP (2001), Vista (2007), Windows 7 (2009)—as dubious adaptations of an inherently flawed design. One of the big problems with Windows, which the Tribe sees as preventable, is that the operating system is especially vulnerable to the predations of malware. Not everyone believes Windows is most-targeted only because it owns the biggest share of the market.

Whatever its alleged failings, and however uncool Microsoft has been made to appear in Apple's clever advertising campaigns, Windows operating systems still run most of the computers in the world, by far. The system itself consists of literally millions of lines of code that support a virtual galaxy of applications, from the profound to the mundane. It's organic, in that it is constantly evolving, and has become far too complex for any one person to fully grasp. The size of the Redmond campus, which employs more than ten thousand people, just over one-tenth of Microsoft's worldwide workforce, reflects this bewildering specialization, with whole divisions of the company, whole sprockets, devoted to a growing variety of software. T.J.'s specialty is protection.

He does not look like a geek. He is tall and athletic, with long arms and legs; broad shoulders; a wide, round clean-shaven face; and rimless glasses. He spent his youth playing sports: baseball, football, soccer—"pretty much anything," he says—and mostly misspent the early years of his college education. Now in his thirties, he still looks like a jock. He has a loose, easy gait and a resolutely informal manner. He wears his hair cropped close, and often covers it with a baseball cap—he was wearing a blue one with the gold initials FBI on the front the day I met him in 2010. The path to his present position was determined not so much by technical interest or ability as by a desire to catch bad guys. Law enforcement was his original goal. He took a somewhat lackadaisical nine-year path through Florida State University in the 1990s, overindulging (by his own account) in the ample social opportunity afforded by the steamy Tallahassee campus before knuckling down to earn an undergraduate degree in criminology, and then a master's degree in information science. The field is only partly related to computers, but T.J. had a stronger than usual relationship with digital networks even then. When graduation appeared on the horizon, he applied for jobs with several federal law enforcement and intelligence agencies. He had his heart set on the CIA, where he might "have an impact," he says, but a friend pointed out that his résumé might also interest a software company.

During his last few years at school, T.J. had a part-time job as an IT (information technology) aide for one of the university's departments. He worked his way up from supporting desktop software to systems manager for the entire department. His parents had gotten him one of the early PCs in the late 1980s, when PCs were starting to become a fixture of home offices, and he had learned enough on it to understand, by the time he went to college, the advantages of linking his computer to the university's large and powerful network. He experimented with using multiple modems to broaden his bandwidth when connecting, and apart from the convenience afforded by the network's speed and accessibility, he discovered caches of new movies and music—places where Internet pirates had stashed their illicit goods. This was a common practice. Video and audio files took up lots of space, so pirates would hack their way into large computer networks and stash their stolen goods in obscure corners where they were likely to go unnoticed. With triple the normal bandwidth, T.J. was able to construct honeypots, where he could study the methodology behind the ever-increasing attacks. He learned a lot about how Internet predators gained access to networks . . . and watched a free movie or two now and then. He was not actually stealing the material, see; it was already stolen. . . . It also gave him a real sense for the emerging world of cybercrime.

His facility with computers and networks landed him a full time IT job, where, between installing machines, checking out applications, and building campus networks, he began dealing with increasingly frequent and sophisticated efforts to break into his department's files. This awakened T.J.'s inner Batman. He learned to apply monitoring tools like port mirrors to snare and track the invaders. Such work was obsessively interesting—toe-to-toe with the villains!—and he was soon more driven by crime fighting than by the routine IT chores or his classes . . . hence his desire to chase bad guys for real as a federal agent. The fed jobs were competitive, particularly after the terrorist attacks of September 11, 2001, fired up patriotic instincts on college campuses, so to cover all his bases T.J. dropped off his résumé with a visting Microsoft recruiter. He didn't even stay for the guy's whole presentation. So he was surprised when he got an email the next day inviting him to drop by for a "screening interview."

Microsoft hired him a few months later, the day before he got married in December, after a grueling daylong round of interviews in Charlotte, North Carolina. The phone call offering him the job delayed his attendance at the rehearsal dinner, but his bride's pique faded quickly when she learned her groom had landed a good job. T.J. progressed rapidly from enterprise-level network support engineering to security work, a growing concern at Microsoft just then. It was a period of rapid growth for malware, and the job handed him the challenge throughout the last decade of matching the miscreants stride for stride.

Much like Microsoft, malware had begun to embrace specialization. Among the new things T.J. saw were prepackaged exploits, essentially break-in vehicles that allowed criminals to load on whatever scam they wished. These exploit kits were marketed to garden-variety spammers and thieves, who no longer needed sophisticated hacking skills to get started. It meant that every newly discovered exploit launched not just one crime, but many, and potentially multiplied the earnings of its inventor many fold—with the added bonus that the exploit itself was not criminal. Prosecuting its creator would be like going after Black & Decker every time a thief used one of its drills to break into a safe. There were highly skilled programmers all over the world probing for a new weakness in Windows, crafting an exploit, and then openly marketing their invention to less tech-savvy crooks.

Botnets were the new big thing. Most Internet scams have a predictable rate of return; the percentage of people fooled into sending money is small, but if the net is cast widely enough, the returns can be large. Microsoft estimates that 5 percent of computer users fall for malware trickery, downloading programs that infect their computers, often despite on-screen warnings not to do so. Some "phishing" attacks on social networks, messages that trick computer operators into revealing valuable personal data or credit card account numbers, have shown a success rate of 70 percent. So an exploit that can guarantee reaching a large enough number of computers is a valuable tool, indeed, more like a license to print money. Nothing is more valuable in this context than a large, stable, secure botnet, a network of vulnerable computers not just accessible but *controlled* by an outside operator. The pressure it mounts on cyberdefenders is unceasing.

It is harder to defend a computer than to attack it. Microsoft's security technicians spend considerable amounts of their time plugging newly discovered holes and issuing "patches" to mend them. This is not scary, esoteric stuff. This is as real as picking a lock, albeit not as simple. Anyone who uses Windows on their home computer is familiar with routine security updates, which Microsoft issues on the second Tuesday of each month. In the Tribe it has become known as "Patch Tuesday."

In September 2008, a group of Chinese hackers began marketing an exploit for $37 that attacked a hitherto unknown weakness at Port 445 of the Windows Operating System. The Chinese hackers were not breaking any laws. They did not attempt any criminal acts. Their product was just a tool for breaking into the heart of a computer running Windows. The first serious effort to use the kit was seen weeks after the kit appeared, in Vietnam, on September 29. A strain of malware dubbed Gimmiv quickly spread from Hanoi to twenty-three nations. Malaysia was hardest hit. Gimmiv was identified by most security experts as a "Trojan," a type of malware that attaches itself to a legitimate program and goes to work when the operator turns it on. The Trojan then copied all of the registry information in the invaded computer, all of its log-on and personal data, and sent it back to the attacker. As a scam, Gimmiv had serious design flaws that limited its effectiveness, but the exploit had worked perfectly. Others were sure to notice. T.J. knew it probably meant a race to exploit the newly discovered vulnerability at Port 445.

Ports are "listening" points in the system, designed to transmit and receive particular kinds of data. There are 65,535 in Windows, because users value speed, so they want their computers to be able to do many things simultaneously. A firewall is a gatekeeper. It sniffs incoming packets of code and either grants or denies or redirects them according to the rules that govern each port. To penetrate the firewall, a packet of code needs to match up with a port; it needs to present itself as something the port is designed to receive. Only certain very specific kinds of data can flow through, and then only with the appropriate codes. Some ports, like Transmission Control Protocol (TCP) 25, which handles email, are heavily trafficked. Most are not; they listen for updates and instructions that deal with narrow and specific functions, usually routine procedures that never rise to the notice of computer users.

The number of ports is determined by TCP and UDP protocols, which are used to trigger the right listening service on the operating system. If a message comes to a port that lacks the right listening service for it, the port is said to be closed, otherwise, the port is open and the computer will receive the message, oftentimes sending a reply to the sender. In Windows, there are a few ports that are open by default unless there is a firewall to control access. One of them is port 445.

On a Windows machine, port 445 triggers a service called Remote Procedure Call (RPC), which allows other computers to print or share files with it. Because of the complexity of the RPC service, the legacy of various generations of Windows, and the intimacy of the service with the heart of the operating system, called the "kernel," there are lots of instances where an error in programming allows an attacker to deliver invalid data, instructions which may cause the service to perform tasks for which it was not intended. This is a problem common to large software systems. A vulnerability in RPC permits a level of control over the computer that a vulnerability in, say, Internet Explorer, would not. Remotely controlling Internet Explorer would enable a miscreant to compel your computer to download pornography or adware, the kind of exploit that is immediately and painfully obvious. Seizing control of the kernel gives a remote operator access deeper than a user would ever see, right to the mind and soul of the computer. He would, effectively, *own* it. At that point the owner of the infected computer has been *pwned,* royally.

The hard part was not entering through Port 445; it was

fooling the operating system into downloading the exploit's malware. To accomplish that, the Chinese kit employed a "buffer overflow," one of the hackers' oldest tricks. It works like this: An outside computer comes knocking at the door with a packet of code. Once it arrives, the operating system needs to find where to put it. So it dispatches a collection of programs called *network services*—think of network services as a "recipe book" that explains how to make various dishes, and the computer as a chef who is avidly reading this book. If the process were simple, the chef would select the correct recipe, or program, and download the new packet. But the process is not simple. Nearly every program involves a variety of subroutines, which interrupt the primary task along the way. These subroutines are, in effect, small packets of memory created within the preexisting memory stack, parentheses within parantheses, like nesting Russian dolls. For example, once the chef chooses what looks like the right recipe from the book, and starts reading, say, from page 73, he is interrupted and told that a remote client has placed an urgent order for a cake. To service the request, the chef immediately flips to the chapter (or program subroutine) that explains how to prepare cakes, say, page 141. But before he digs into the cake recipe, he creates a temporary memory stack—call it an addendum to the cake recipe—and places a bookmark there, called a "pointer," to remind him where he left off (page 73), and where he needs to return once the cake is baked. Then he sets about making the cake, which has its own subroutines, like, say, contacting the customer to find out whether he wants angel food or chocolate.

Here is where the malware programmer performs his trick. He is the cake customer. He gives the chef a list of his requirements for the cake, and he knows from previous observation that these instructions will be placed by the chef in an addendum, or the temporary stack, which is called a buffer. The evil programmer knows exactly how big that buffer is. So, in addition to giving the chef details of the cake he wants, he continues to feed the chef unrelated information. If the chef is undiscerning, as Port 445 proved to be, the superfluous data will overflow the allotted buffer space and spill into the addendum, so that the chef inadvertently overwrites his pointer, the one telling him to return to page 73 when he is finished. Instead, the cake instructions now send him in an entirely new direction, like, say, telling the chef—who is a very literal-minded fellow and follows instructions like . . . a machine!—to fetch a key and open a safe he keeps in a back room. This information, which has nothing to do with cake instructions, is duly recorded at the bottom of the addendum. So when the chef finishes with the cake, and checks his addendum to know where he needs to return, he is directed back not to page 73, but to the back room and the safe.

If the right check is in place, the computer at that point would simply reject the incoming packet, or complain— send up a specific warning message to the computer user that only very few comprehend. There are ways for the service to check to see if the space it allocated is large enough or if an attacker has successfully written too much information, either of which would abort the invasion. But the service must do that at every single point, and there could be thousands of such points in a complex program like RPC. The Chinese discovered one point that wasn't adequately protected. So instead of the RPC service simply aborting the process and shutting down the buffer, just as the handle of a gas pump will automatically shut down when the tank is full, the computer, or chef, continues processing the data along this new and unauthorized path.

This is the essence of the exploit. Like all programs, network services list data and instructions, a set of procedures that the computer follows faithfully. The invading code now steers its malware package wherever the programmer has told it to go, and because Port 445 is buried deep in the operating system, the payoff for an intrusion there is big. The lock has been picked.

Microsoft learned of this new exploit as soon as the Chinese hackers began selling it, and recognized that it potentially posed a major threat. It was "wormable," that is, it was the kind of attack that would allow for the insertion of a worm, which could then propagate itself into a botnet. It could execute a "remote procedure call": in other words, the computer could be handed over to a remote operator. The threat was serious enough that the company decided to issue its hastily designed patch for this vulnerability, MS08-067 (Microsoft 2008—Patch 67), "out of band," that is, it decided not to wait until the next "Patch Tuesday."

T.J. was at a four-day International Botnet Task Force meeting in Arlington, Virginia, hosted at Carnegie-Mellon University on October 23, 2008, when MS08-067 was announced and made available for download. The timing gave him a chance to explain it in person to some of the top security researchers in the world. When the final decision was relayed to him from Redmond, he stood up with his associate Richie Lai to announce it.

"Hey, I want everybody to go onto Microsoft.com, slash, technet, slash, security," he said. "There's an out-of-band release."

The company release accompanying the patch explained: "On Microsoft Windows 2000, Windows XP, and Windows Server 2003 systems, an attacker could exploit this vulnerability without authentication to run arbitrary code. It is possible that this vulnerability could be used in the crafting of a wormable exploit."

Many at the meeting downloaded the patch immediately and began dissecting it. T.J. spent the next few minutes explaining it and answering questions, and then met with people from the FBI to brief them the same afternoon.

"We think this is going to be a big deal," he told the agents. "You guys really need to start looking at that."

In a perfect world, the patch would end the problem. But

as T.J. well knew, MS08-067 was more likely to makes things worse. Anyone who downloaded it would be protected from the exploit, so Microsoft had to release it in order to protect its most diligent customers. But the patch itself was better advertising than the Chinese hackers could ever afford. It was like placing in orbit a flashing neon billboard so gaudy that it could be seen everywhere on Earth with the naked eye—*Come one! Come all! A new Windows vulnerability!*

In fact, the patch itself most likely inspired the new worm's creation. Many, many computer operators worldwide fail to diligently heed security updates. Millions of "Windows" systems around the world have been bootlegged, counterfeited, or installed without authorization. If everyone registered his software and applied new patches promptly, Windows would be nigh impregnable. But because so many people fail to do so, "Patch Tuesday," or in this case an out-of-band patch, has become part of Microsoft's problem. It is as if the commander of a fort made a public announcement—"The back door to the supply shed in the southeast corner of the garrison has a broken lock; here's how to fix it." If there were only one well-policed fort, the lock would be fixed and the vulnerability would disappear. But when you are defending millions of forts, and a goodly number snooze right through the public announcement, the patches simply point out the unlocked door. They don't just invite attack; they provide instructions!

This was scary stuff if you allowed yourself to really think about it, which few did. It pointed up a flaw in the founding *let's join hands and sing!* techno-utopian spirit of the Internet itself, a flaw so basic that it could not be fixed. It suggested some kind of social equivalence to entropy, an unbendable curve toward ruin. It was proof, as if further proof were needed, that nothing works exactly as intended.

Making computers easy for everyone to use was the germ of the idea that made Bill Gates and Paul Allen into two of the richest men in the world, but by inviting everybody to the computer revolution, they threw open the doors to the technologically ignorant, which is to say, most of us. This would prove to be enormously frustrating in later years to those who understood most and cared most about the Internet. If everyone would only take simple precautions . . . but that was *never going to happen.* It had been tough enough to get users to pay attention when malware was primitive, when it stomped in with muddy boots and ground its heels into their hard drives. How were you going to get them to pay attention when the malware was so stealthy that only the most alert and well-trained technician could detect it? When the thing to be protected was not so much the individual PC as the Internet itself? People simply would never understand, and even if they did, they lacked discipline. In a free society, you could not reach in and update their software for them— just imagine the howls of indignation, the bad PR, the class-action lawsuits! Big Brother tickling the innards of your very own machine? It was about as clear a violation of the techno-utopian ideal as could be imagined. The implication was that this billion-headed, globally connected marvel would always be vulnerable, and not just to predation. It could be weaponized. It could be crippled or even crashed at the whim of some technically proficient cybergang or perhaps even by some borderline Asperger's teenager who woke up on the wrong side of the bed. And even when you did everything right, even when you anticipated the exploit and turned out the patch in record time, *it just made things worse!*

Sure enough, as soon as MSO8-067 appeared, demand for the Chinese exploit kit grew so fast that its creators began giving it away. There was a new outbreak of Gimmiv in Asia. Security experts were not too worried about Gimmiv, which was amateurish, but they could see the potential.

"If the bad people find out how to use this, we're in big trouble," wrote Eric Sites, a researcher for Sunbelt, a security software firm. He warned that a better-designed piece of malware, like a worm, "could be created very easily and wreak havoc."

Twenty-eight days after MS08-067 appeared, the very thing popped up on Phil Porras's Infections Log at SRI, and started burrowing its way into unprotected computers everywhere.

And nobody, nobody, was less surprised than T. J. Campana.

3

REMOTE THREAD INJECTION

"IF HE CAME HERE IT WAS FOR A REASON."
"A DARKER REASON THAN YOU CAN IMAGINE, SIR."
—The Amazing X-Men

Hassen Saidi took it personally when the worm shrugged off SRI's unpacking software.

The tool to pry open malware, to slice right through the layers of protective and deceptive coding, had been created by Hassen, along with Monirul Sharif, a graduate assistant. They called it Eureka. Any malware that resisted it was a personal challenge, and an opportunity to improve Eureka.

Hassen is the data flow analyst on Phil Porras's staff. He is a native of Algeria who migrated to Menlo Park after earning his doctorate in computer science in France. He's firmly in the Internet idealist camp. He sees the web as one of the most revolutionary developments in human history, and regards the efforts of criminals, nihilists, and terrorists to prey on it as reprehensible. More and more, the world as we know it depends on the smooth interaction of computers. The Internet has become the collective mind of humanity, its eyes and ears and memory. As old paper repositories convert to digital storage, and as the new trail of modern civilization increasingly inhabits the digital realm, it has become, in a sense, the new Library of Alexandria. Better than most, security pros like Hassen recognize how easy it would be to burn it down.

At the dawn of the computer age, hackers were mostly a nuisance, motivated by a desire to show off. Today the most serious computer predators are funded by rich criminal syndicates and even nation-states, and their goals are far more ambitious. Cyberattacks were launched at digital networks in Estonia by ethnic Russian protesters in 2007 and in Georgia before Russia attacked that country in 2008; and someone, probably Israel or the United States (or both), successfully loosed a worm called Stuxnet in 2010 to sabotage computer-controlled uranium centrifuges inside Iran's secretive nuclear program. Botnets have been employed in lucrative global scams and syndicates. In October 2010, the Zeus Trojan, a kit that can be used to create a botnet, has been responsible for infecting nearly four million computers in the United States alone. One Zeus-based scam was discovered to have plundered more than $70 million from the bank accounts of tens of thousands of unwitting victims. Those behind such efforts are often every bit as skilled as those charged with stopping them. The two sides in this war are fellow members of the Geek

Tribe engaged in a highly cerebral and esoteric contest at the cutting edge of computer programming.

The stakes are high. Staying one step ahead of the botmaster, the "miscreants," or "bad guys," or "black hats," as the security community dubs them, is a constant challenge. The obscure work these experts do, the work that is so hard for most people to understand, may not be as romantic or physically daring as the work of the pilots who flew those fighters on Phil Porras's office wall, or the assault force in 2011 that killed Osama Bin Laden in Pakistan, but it is every bit as vital and compelling. The threat may be virtual, but the consequences would be all too real. A successful computer attack could compromise nuclear reactors, electrical grids, transportation networks, pipelines—you name it. Earlier this year, the Pentagon formulated its first-ever formal cyberstrategy, which found that a cyberattack on the United States originating in another country would be considered as much an act of war as dropping bombs on Buffalo, one that would justify a traditional military response. It is, of course, always easier to tear something down than to build it up, easier to break into a computer than to protect it, so the good guys work at a constant disadvantage. The tide of malware is relentless. Battling it without losing heart requires both steadfast resolve and, at some level, faith in man's essential goodness.

With dark semicircles under his big brown eyes, Hassen has the look of the creature Weizenbaum sketched back in

1976, a man who spends too many hours bathed in the light of a computer screen. He is forty, with thick brown curls that have begun to gray at the temples. His aptitude and learning have been seasoned with decades of experience. He has honed one very specific skill to a fine art. If he is not the best at what he does, he would like to know who is.

Hassen pursued computer studies in part to avoid direct competition within his accomplished family. His father is a professor of literature and his mother an elementary school teacher. Five of his siblings have earned PhDs in various disciplines. Two of his older brothers were mathematicians, so when he graduated from high school he decided to go a different way. The math brothers advised computer science, a growing field with plenty of opportunities for both study and employment, and Hassen heeded them, even though he had no particular love for computers, a circumstance that makes him different from most of those working at his level. After SRI recruited him from the French lab, he spent several years in Menlo Park focusing on programming languages and computer reliability, but realized gradually that the real action was in the malware wars. He talked his way into the job, convincing Phil that his cutting-edge programming skills were ideally suited to dissecting the newest strains of malware. Nowadays when people ask him what he does for a living, he says, "I track criminals."

If they press for more detail, he'll confess that his crime fighting is relegated to the virtual space inside SRI's computer network, "tracking viruses." Further explanation produces the Glaze.

"At that point," he says, "they're not interested."

But how could anything be more interesting? A malicious program that appears impervious to dissection is the handiwork of someone, or some group, trying to prey on honest citizens in the global community, which is to say that the predator is trying, ultimately, to outsmart *him*. Hassen is that rare program analyst who is comfortable working not just with source code, any of the many programming languages, but with "object code," the long strings of ones and zeros at the core of machine instruction. At that primary layer, a program's intent cannot be disguised or obfuscated. Once Hassen sinks his teeth into a piece of malware, the question is not *if* he can unpack and dissect it, but how long it will take him to do so.

What makes it hard, and what makes Hassen's world so devilishly difficult to understand, is not just the complexity of modern computer operating systems, but the fact that much of what takes place inside them can be grasped and described only conceptually. Software is abstract. It's also very real, of course, but not real the way an internal combustion engine is real. Inside an operating system there are no visible moving parts. It is a world of electromagnetic charges orchestrated to move along pathways that make decisions and create "memory." There are many levels of memory, from the kind that sticks around on a hard drive forever to the kind that is so evanescent it exists for only microseconds, for as long as it takes a computer to step through some lightning-fast computation.

Every program is ultimately a list of instructions written in the ones and zeros of object code, which represent slightly different electrical charges. It breaks down complex tasks into a series of steps so basic that they can be expressed in a long series of binary decisions, or logic gates, which are executed by the computer's central processing unit (CPU). The art of programming is breaking complex tasks into these fundamental steps. It is maddeningly precise work, because computers are maddeningly literal. Bill Gates once said, "Most great programmers have some mathematical background, because it helps to have studied the purity of proving theorems, where you don't make soft statements, you only make precise statements." Say, for instance, your body was a machine with a CPU, which, in a sense, it is, and you wished to stand up from a chair, walk across the room, and fix a cup of coffee. You would begin by telling each of the dozens of muscles involved in rising from a seated position to perform their functions, flex or relax, while monitoring balance readings from your inner ear and rerouting orders for muscular adjustments to make sure you don't fall over sideways. By the time you have walked across the room, reached up to remove a cup from the cupboard, picked up the coffeepot, etc., you have executed a blizzard of binary decisions. The various source codes, or computer languages, are shorthand versions of object code, designed to make a program accessible to human programmers. If standing up and crossing the room and pouring a cup of coffee constitute a routine task, it might be rendered in source code simply as "get coffee," which automatically refers the CPU to a standard predetermined sequence (we have all experienced the sensation of performing quotidian tasks on autopilot). But in order to perform even the simplest of tasks, the computer, just like the mind of a man crossing the room to pour a cup of coffee, must remember things, sometimes for split seconds, sometimes for longer. To make the cup of coffee we must access core memories, like which ingredients to mix and in what amounts, or how to operate the coffeemaker; and to stand and cross the room, to lift and to pour, we must create transient memories, like those continual readings from the inner ear to maintain balance. Inside the operating system of a modern computer there are similar multilayered memory functions operating simultaneously, along pathways meticulously prescribed by the program.

To understand this new worm, either Hassen had to set it running and carefully observe it step by step, a dynamic analysis; or he had to, in effect, unspool its programming language so that he could read it, step by painstaking step, a static analysis. But first he had to find it. The worm may have been cunningly packed, but if it was to do its thing inside its host, the infected computer itself had to recognize how to open it. If you could watch that happen, step by step, you would learn how to unpack it yourself. But where inside the operating system of a newly infected computer did the worm hatch?

Malware is packed for two reasons. First, for compression, because to disseminate widely around the Internet the data packet needs to be small. Second, for self-protection, to make it harder for antivirus software to recognize it and for someone like Hassen to take it apart and study it. The worm itself consisted of only a few hundred lines of code, no more than thirty-five kilobytes, slightly smaller than a two-thousand-word document. The average home computer today has about two gigabytes of memory, well over 1.5 million times greater. If you were not looking for it, and unless you knew *how* to look for it, you would never see it. The worm drifts in like a mote. In order to prevent the kind of analysis Hassen wished to perform, its designers had made it particularly hard to follow once it entered a new machine. They had, in effect, covered the worm's tracks, and they had provided a false trail to throw pursuers off the scent. They also applied a dual-layer encryption method, like Russian nesting dolls, capable of defeating most unpacking software and security ninjas.

Most.

Hassen is not easily fooled. He minutely traced the code's tricky pathway into his virtual computer. The worm used the Chinese Exploit to enter Port 445, taking advantage of the buffer overflow to write itself in as a Dynamic-Link Library (DLL)—the device Microsoft programmers crafted to enable computers to exchange data. Regular users know nothing about program languages or varying exchange protocols. They just want the thing to run. So Microsoft invented a way to bundle executable programs and data, the DLL, that allows them to be smoothly exchanged by computers on different networks. Once inside, the worm (now a DLL) proceeded along a standard path. It was directed to *svchost.exe* (short for "Service Host"), which is a check-in point for incoming files of this type. *Svchost* then ran its "LoadLibrary," function, which does what it says it does: it uploads the new file.

If the worm served some legitimate function, it would then have been initialized and handed over to the computer user, or it would have failed to initialize and been given the boot. The latter is what appeared to happen. When the DLL timed out, *svchost* raised an exception and aborted the load. This was the false trail. There was nothing to suggest anything more had happened. To most people, even those monitoring the system very carefully, the incoming packet had failed to initialize and was now gone.

Of course, as Hassen well knew, the worm was not gone. It had performed a nasty trick. The first-level unpacking at *svchost* had released nesting dolls, not one but *two* distinct packets: one for code, another for data.

The data packet functioned the way you would expect; it informed the system that it was incompatible, and that it had self-destructed. The other, the code packet, opened up a memory—a protected memory segment—and then decrypted and installed itself. It pushed that segment off as a "remote thread," that is, a hidden code that executes itself within the address space of an existing, legitimate process. Thus hidden, it injected itself under a random file name into the Windows root directory, a file called *services. exe,* which runs background applications. At this point, the worm *owned* the computer. It had pulled up a chair in the very core of the operating system, the innermost kernel, what amounted to the system's medulla, which is the lower portion of your brain that regulates autonomous functions like the in-out of your breathing, the opening and closing of the ventricles in your heart, and the contractions of the slippery linings of your intestines. Human beings operate their bodies in the sense that they can will themselves to run a sub-four-minute mile or pull an all-nighter before a chemistry test, but the really important controls, the life-and-death functions, are buried too deep for conscious control. They are safely beyond the reach of clumsy, changeable willpower. The root directory for an operating system is likewise hidden away. Computer operators who inadvertently stumble on it are sternly warned, in so many words, *Don't mess with this unless you really know what you are doing!*

Hassen traced these steps with great care, until he was able to find and isolate the remote thread inside his virtual computer, and attach it to his own executable file. At that point he had the worm, in effect, splayed out on his dissection table. He could turn it on and watch it actually go to work. The program's code was deliberately obfuscated, making it more difficult than usual to read, but over several weeks, looking at long strings of ones and zeros, Hassen managed to piece it together. One of the first things he learned was that the botnet being assembled by the worm was scheduled to wake up on November 26. Whoever launched it had given it six days to spread before activation. Because the worm kept track of time by checking with the host computer's clock, Hassen could get an advance look at what it had in store simply by turning his computer's internal clock forward.

One of the first things it did surprised him. After performing a few routine moves to initiate itself, disabling the computer's antivirus programs (the infected computer could no longer receive security updates from anti-malware companies), patching the vulnerability at Port 445 (the smart burglar closes and locks the window he entered), and opening a back door through the computer's firewall to enable it to make an outbound connection from the victimized computer to the botmaster, the worm then checked to see if its new host had a Ukrainian keyboard. That was unusual, and revealing. The Internet is global, but law enforcement is not. In many countries, and the Ukraine is one, there is no law against deploying computer scams against people in other countries. So long as cyberthieves do not prey on Ukrainian citizens, they could theoretically empty the bank accounts of every American citizen without breaking the law in their home country (incidentally, there was a large Ukrainian community in Buenos Aires, where the worm had apparently originated). If the worm discovered a Ukrainian keyboard on the machine, it would not install itself. If it did not, it proceeded.

Next, it contacted a website called *maxmind.com* and downloaded a Geographic Internet Protocol (GeoIP) database. This is what Phil had noted in the original readout on his Infections Log. The geo data told the worm both where it was and where the computers it sought to infect were. There were at least two reasons why this information might be useful. It could have been yet another way to avoid Ukrainian machines, but it also made the worm's propagation more efficient. Exploiting a buffer overflow is tricky. By knowing where the targeted computer was located, the sender could tailor the message appropriately.

Once it established where the infected machine was, once it learned its IP address, the worm contacted the machine's Internet Service Provider (ISP) and began scanning all machines on the same network for vulnerabilities—looking for Windows Operating Systems to infect. If the machine initially infected was part of a large network, say, at a university or military complex, it is likely that none of the other machines on that network were patched, so the worm spread very rapidly within networks. For a machine connected to a commercial Internet provider the process went more slowly, because there was less uniformity of operating systems on the machines that used that ISP. But once a single machine was infected, every IP address on that network was potentially vulnerable.

After it performed these steps, the worm rested. God took a full day. The worm rested for just thirty minutes.

It is doubtful at this point that any normal computer user would notice the infection. The worm so limited its use of the host computer's resources and network bandwidth that it barely registered any activity. This was a highly effective method of hiding. So long as the normal functions of the computer seem unchanged—and they would *seem* unchanged even if slowed by a few microseconds—most computer users would not think to look for an infection. Fussy users who are aware of the normal bandwidth of their machine, the measure of the rate of data exchange, might notice an infection if the rate suddenly increased. This worm was so efficient that its operation registered only slightly on bandwidth monitors, so even users who made a practice of checking the bits-per-second flow of their machines would be unlikely to notice a significant change.

All of this was clever enough, but most of these moves had come before in the world of malware. They marked this worm as state of the art. What Hassen saw next as he peeled still deeper really impressed him. Its designers were, in a very real sense, his enemy, but while he might deplore the motives and character of those who unloosed this worm, he could not help admiring their craft.

On November 26 all infected computers would begin checking to see if their host computer was connected to the Internet, and if so, would begin trying to call home. The worm would begin by generating a list of seemingly random Internet domain names, 250 of them, every three hours. Every like-infected computer in the world would perform the same trick, spitting out the same 250 addresses every three hours until the end of the day. The next day it would create an entirely new list of 250 domain names. If the host computer was off-line, it would check back every minute until it could resume the exercise. The worm-generated domains appeared random, just meaningless strings of numbers and letters followed by one of five Top Level Domain (TLD) indicators— *.com, .org, .net, .info,* or *.biz*—but they were, in fact, entirely predictable if you knew the algorithm that produced them. Whoever was controlling the worm needed only to be behind one of those 250 doors to issue a command.

Phoning home had always been a botnet's biggest weakness. Worms that created botnets were designed to do four basic things: to break into a computer, to secure it from further security updates, to spread, and to call home for instructions. Without receiving further instructions, the invader was harmless. It carried no instructions of its own beyond installing itself securely (all of the functions Hassen observed were designed to settle the invader in safely) and spreading. Once all of the infected computers started calling in for instructions, the worm was vulnerable. If the white hats could find the right domain name of the controller, they could contact a registrar and have it blocked or taken down (and supply law enforcement authorities with the culprit's home office). Effectively, the botnet would be dead. But with 250 new domains being generated every day, this was not going to be an easy task. Whoever had designed this one knew something about how the white hats worked, and had planned ahead . . .

In more ways than one. Because if someone figured out which door the botmaster was waiting behind on a given day, this worm was programmed to communicate in code, and not just in any code. Whoever designed it was concerned about more than being thwarted by the good guys. The designers were also worried about competing criminals. A secure botnet was a valuable tool. If a rival botmaster could determine its command and control site and issue his own instructions, he could effectively steal it. So the new worm took no chances. It employed the most advanced public encryption method in existence to protect its communications.

Breaking codes used to be the province of clever puzzle masters, who during World War II devised encryption and code-breaking methods so difficult that operators needed machines to do the work. Computers today can perform so many calculations so fast that, theoretically, there is no longer any such thing as an unbreakable code. One applies what computer scientists call "brute force": trying every possible combination systematically until the secret is revealed. Such an approach would take human beings thousands of years if the code was sufficiently complex, but it would take a modern computer only a few seconds. The encryption game today is about making a cipher so difficult that the amount of brute force required to break it renders the effort pointless, or too expensive —the "thief" would have to spend more to obtain the prize than the prize is worth. In his 1999 history of code-making and -breaking, *The Code Book,* Simon Singh wrote: "It is now routine to encrypt a message [so securely] that all the computers on the planet would need longer than the age of the universe to break the cipher."

It is one thing to write a code that only its controller can decipher, but quite another to devise a method for two parties to communicate in code, in public. Public encryption is essential for, among other things, e-commerce, where customers send private information over the Internet.

The basis for the highest-level is a public-encryption method invented in 1977 by three researchers at MIT: Ron Rivest (the primary author), Israeli cryptographer Adi Shamir, and Leonard Adleman of the University of

Southern California. In the more than thirty years since it was devised, the method has been improved several times. The National Institute of Standards and Technology sets the Federal Information Processing Standard, which defines the cryptography algorithms that government agencies must use to protect communications. It is also the basis for nearly all high-level encryption that allows private transactions over the Internet. The American standard is determined by an international competition among the world's top cryptologists, and since this is the highest-level contest of its kind, the winning entry becomes the world's standard by default. The current high-level standard is labeled Secure Hash Algorithm–2 (SHA-2).

The worm used three crypto algorithms. It utilized Rivest Cipher 4 (RC4) to encrypt its binary messages; SHA512 (one of the family of high-level standards that use 512-bit words) to ensure that even if someone broke the RC4 cipher the intruder would not be able to alter the message, because the algorithm would detect a single-bit modification in a trillion-bit stream; and RSA (Rivest, Shamir, Adleman), a signature system that guaranteed messages from the worm's controller were authentic. The use of RSA meant that both the worm and the botmaster possessed two keys, a 1,024-bit public key and a 1,024-bit private key. The worm's keys were different from the botmaster's keys. In order to break the code, you needed both. The worm sent its message encrypted with the botmaster's public key, and he could decrypt it with his private key. A return message would be encrypted with the worm's public key, but could be decrypted only with its private one. It was theoretically possible to divine the private key from the public key, but only with one of the most powerful computers in the world, like, say, the ones available to the National Security Agency (NSA) or the Defense Department. Even if Phil and his team succeeded in intercepting a message from the botmaster, they would not be able to decode it.

This meant the worm's author or authors were fluent at the highest levels of cryptography. As exceptional as this step was, Hassen had seen it before. It did show an unusual degree of care. These people were clever, he thought; they had designed this with a checklist in mind. They had done their homework. They were not just creating a remarkable illicit asset; they were determined to protect it, keeping one step ahead of whoever might compromise it.

That was impressive, but the next thing Hassen saw as he peeled deeper into the worm really surprised him. He had never seen it before. On the *http* query line for each generated web address, each of those random domain names it generated daily, was a number that at first he did not comprehend. He shelved the question for a few weeks as he worked out how to dial the Domain Generating Algorithm (DGA) forward, generating a daily calendar of the websites the worm would be trying to contact. But when he had finished with that, he returned to the number.

He finally determined that it recorded the number of machines the worm had infected from that bot. He saw immediately why that would be useful. The worm was randomly infecting any machine it could infect, but some computers were more interconnected than others. Most of us live and work within a relatively small circle of people, so our computers interact with only a small number of others. But some people, and hence some computers, are what social network theorists call "nodes." They are widely connected. They tend to be on the Internet full-time. They exchange information with an extraordinarily large number of others. The mystery number on the *http* line informed the botmaster which computers on its net were the most widely connected, and the most valuable. This meant that if the white hats succeeded in shutting the botnet down, its creators would not have to start over with random infections; they could begin by targeting the nodes, which would propagate the worm much more efficiently and quickly. That, thought Hassen, was "really, really clever." These guys were creating this botnet *to last*.

The new worm was to do something else on November 26. It was programmed to contact a notorious malware distributor called *TrafficConverter.biz*. This site offered "affiliates" cash for steering suckers its way. Each unsuspecting computer owner conned into linking with the site began receiving bogus warnings of infection on his screen that directed him to download antivirus software, which sold for anywhere from $50 to $75. The real infection, of course, was *TrafficConverter*'s program, which blocked the computer user from contacting legitimate antivirus companies and would continually pester the user until he paid the fee. The site's operators offered prizes for affiliates who brought in the most business, including a Lexus sports sedan. Huge amounts of money were made this way, both by the owners of *TrafficConverter.biz* and by its affiliates, who were raking in as much as $3.9 million a year, according to a report by cybersecurity reporter Brian Krebs.

But two days before the new worm was scheduled to steer its botnet to the scam, *TrafficConverter.biz* was taken down. Major credit card companies had suspended payment operations for the site, effectively putting it out of business. This turned out to be best for all concerned, including *TrafficConverter.biz*, because when the worm kicked in, it steered *83 million inquiries* to the site from 179,000 unique IP addresses. This would have crashed the site if it had been open for business.

At first glance, the connection with *TrafficConverter.biz* suggested a lead to the worm's authors. About a month before the worm appeared, another notorious malware distributor, Baka Software, had sponsored a contest. It offered a new car to whoever could infect the most computers. Baka was responsible for a scam called "Antivirus XP," and, as it happens, this was likely to have been the product downloaded by computers that contacted *TrafficConverter.biz*. The company also has a registered office in Kiev.

The connection suggested that the new worm's designers might have been trying to win the contest. If the website had not been taken down, the worm would have steered an unprecedented flood of business its way—too much, as it happened. But there were other possibilities. Since the traffic generated by the new worm would have crashed the site, might it have been designed by *TrafficConverter.biz*'s competition? Or were the new worm's creators toying with the white hats, creating a false trail, much as they had done with the packaging of the worm itself? Why not cover their tracks further by drawing everyone's attention to a known malware distributor who was, in this case, innocent?

Whatever its purpose, the link to *TrafficConverter.biz* gave the worm a name. Some labs had been calling it "Downadup" or "Kido," but Microsoft security programmers shuffled the letters of *trafficconverter* and came up with "Conficker." *Ficken* is the German word for "fuck." Blend that with English syntax and you get *ficker,* which this worm was, without a doubt.

The name stuck.

By December 1, Conficker had burrowed into an estimated 500,000 computers worldwide and was knocking out 250 new domains every day looking for instructions.

It was just getting started.

4

AN OCEAN
OF SUCKERS

HAVING MUTANT POWERS DOESN'T GIVE US
THE RIGHT TO DOMINATE OTHERS.
—The X-Men Chronicles

The idea of an infectious computer "worm" is lifted from the pages of science fiction. More than a decade before the Internet was born, the British sci-fi writer John Brunner invented the idea of a viral code that could invade and sabotage it in his 1975 novel *The Shockwave Rider*.

With startling foresight, at a time when Bill Gates was taking a leave of absence from Harvard to cofound "Micro-Soft," Brunner imagined a dystopian twenty-first-century world wired into a global "data-net," controlled by a malicious state. His hero, a gifted hacker named Nick Haflinger, creates a program he calls a "tapeworm" that can infiltrate the data-net, spread on its own, and ultimately subvert the government. "My newest—my masterpiece—breeds by itself," he boasts. In Haflinger's case, much as with the creators of Wikileaks, the data-net is directed to break into government files and spill state secrets. Brunner chose to call his techno-weapon a "tapeworm" because the code, like the creature, consisted of a head attached to a string of segments that were each capable of regenerating the whole.

"What I turned loose in the net yesterday was the father and mother of all tapeworms . . . it can't be killed," he says. "It's indefinitely self-perpetuating so long as the net exists. . . . Incidentally, though, it won't expand to indefinite size and clog the net for other use. It has built-in limits. . . . Though I say so myself, it's a neat bit of work."

Brunner's ideas about the coming digital world were clever, but as a prophet he was strictly derivative. His vision was of a piece with those of George Orwell, Aldous Huxley, Philip K. Dick, and others who foresaw the totalitarian movements of the twentieth century as portents of a dark future, where all power would be concentrated in the hands of an oppressive state. Each of these writers predicted that technology would be an important tool of state oppression—for Orwell it was TV, for Huxley it was psychotropic drugs, for Dick it was both of the above combined with bioengineering. For Brunner it was the computer, or, more correctly, computer networks. The ideas in *The Shockwave Rider,* particularly those about the coming age of digital interconnection, were largely based on futurist

Alvin Toffler's book *Future Shock*. They were so prescient that computer programmers recalled the "tapeworm" a few years later when they began devising the first real worms in research labs.

The fears Orwell, Huxley, Dick, and Brunner vividly articulated in their fiction still have adherents, and have inspired some striking and successful Hollywood films, but so far they have not panned out, certainly not in the case of computer networks. The structure of the Internet—or *lack* of structure—has worked against centralized state control. The thing has a billion heads. It is defiantly ground-up. Since it has become a factor in world events, governments everywhere have found it harder to keep secrets and to escape the public's gaze. The "data-net" has proved so far to be a tool less of oppression than of liberation. And the architects of worms and viruses aren't the heroic rebels battling state tyranny imagined by Brunner, but nihilists and common criminals.

In the mid-1970s, the only large computer networks that existed were at university, business, or government centers. Many of the young computer geeks who would create the Internet age, and in some cases amass great fortunes, first stumbled into the larger potential for such networks by borrowing processing time (with or without permission) to play games or show off their hacking skills. Gates and Allen used the computer provided to privileged students at Lakeside Prep, and when they outgrew it they persuaded the school to lease time for them on an outside one. There were few barriers to access, because computing power and connectivity were seen as entirely beneficial. Openness was essential to the movement's appeal.

The first sour notes in this techno-Eden were simple devilry. The early computer networks were plagued by savvy outlaws, "cyberpunks," who used their knowledge of operating systems to play pranks, to write juvenile slogans across the monitors of compromised computers the way graffiti artists scrawl their initials on urban walls. There was a playful quality to such efforts, undertaken often just to show off the hacker's skill. The term was not entirely derogatory. Hackers took some pride in the designation, and had fans. Most of what they did was harmless. To this day the grungy long-haired geek living in his parents' basement, fueled by pizza, soda, and junk food—the picture first painted by Weizenbaum—has become a cliché in Hollywood, bedeviling the powerful with his antisocial genius, thwarting malevolent syndicates, running rings around the "official" experts. These pioneer miscreants came to symbolize the anarchic spirit of the Internet movement, the maverick genius at war with the establishment.

But as the Inernet has rapidly evolved, so have its predators. The newness of computer networks, and their global nature, posed novel problems for law enforcement. In many jurisdictions, preying on people in cyberspace is not officially criminal, and often in places where it is, there is little urgency in prosecuting it. In his 1989 best seller, *The Cuckoo's Egg,* Cliff Stoll told the story of his stubborn, virtually single-handed hunt for an elusive hacker in Germany who was sneaking around inside Stoll's computer network at the Lawrence Berkeley National Laboratory and using it as a back door to U.S. Defense Department computers. The subject was hunted down but never prosecuted, in part because there were no clear laws against such behavior. For many people, *The Cuckoo's Egg* introduced the netherworld of gamesmanship that still defines computer security. Stoll's hacker never penetrated the most secret corners of the national-security net, and even relatively serious breaches like the one Stoll described were still more of a nuisance than a threat. A group calling itself the Legion of Doom had a good run in the 1990s, invading computer networks and showing off while not doing much damage. The group published a technical newsletter to advertise its exploits, and members gave themselves colorful comic-book-style monikers. There were other hacker groups like it, including the New York–based Masters of Deception. Some members of these clubs were hauled in and prosecuted by federal authorities in the 1990s, considerably upping the price of such stunts. Little of the old glamour still attaches itself to serious hackers; the game has evolved into something far bigger, smarter, and more menacing.

Real trouble arrived with the big DDoS (Distributed Denial of Service) attacks of the 1990s, which aimed tidal waves of service requests at certain websites. Instead of showcasing the skill of a hacker, the purpose of a DDoS attack was wholly malicious, sometimes political, often vengeful. A DDoS attack capitalizes on the openness of Internet traffic to simply overwhelm the capacity of an organization to respond. Those orchestrating such attacks employed computer networks to automatically generate request after request, multiple times per second, until they brought to a halt the servers for credit card companies, banks, the White House, government agencies, the Holocaust Historical Museum, political parties, universities, and any other vulnerable website that was deemed offensive. The worst DDoS attack came on October 21, 2002, when the Internet's thirteen root servers were hit simultaneously. This was clearly an effort to bring down not just individual websites, but the Internet itself. The root servers survived the hourlong assault, but only barely. It forced such root servers to invest in heavily redundant stores of memory, enough to absorb massive potential attacks.

This event was important. It was a sobering demonstration for those paying attention, which is to say, the Tribe. This was a very small, select group of people. The vast majority of Internet users remained oblivious. So long as Google and YouTube and Facebook kept humming along, everyone else was happy. By the twenty-first century, the Internet was a given. It was there on your phone, in your car, on your iPad. It was everywhere, through either a WiFi or a phone connection. There were myths about its invulnerability. It could not be shut down, because it lacked any kind of central control or routing system, or so the story went . . . and there was some truth to that belief. The way the Internet routed information *was* entirely new, an advance over all previous communications systems, and one that was inherently sturdier.

Finding your way on the Internet isn't as direct as, say, routing a telephone call. Telephone lines carry the electrical impulses of an outgoing call along wires down the shortest available path to the number being called. The big difference between the Internet and telephone networks, or the interstate highway system, for that matter, is that traffic does not flow down clearly defined, predictable pathways. There are detailed printed maps of telephone networks and highways, and the paths taken by calls and vehicles can always be clearly traced. One of the major conceptual breakthoughs that enabled the creation of the Internet was to do away with this clarity.

The idea was called "packet-switching." The concept apparently came almost simultaneously to two cold war scientists: Donald Davies, working at Britian's National National Physical Laboratory; and an American immigrant scientist from Poland named Paul Baran, at the RAND Corporation in the late 1960s. Both researchers were trying to invent a new, more robust communications network.

Baran was specifically tasked with designing one that might withstand a nuclear attack. Davies was just just looking for an improvement over the existing telephone switching networks, but there is little doubt that experience of prolonged German aerial bombardment during World War II lurked somewhere in the back of his mind. Traditional phone networks had critical trunk lines and central switching stations that, if destroyed, could effectively short-circuit the entire network. Both Baran and Davies wanted a system that could survive such blows, that could not be *taken out*. The alternative that seemed to work best was modeled after the human brain.

Neurologists knew that after severe head injuries, the brain began to power up alternative neural pathways that avoided areas of damaged or destroyed cells. Often patients completely recovered functions that, at first glance, might have seemed hopelessly lost. The brain seemed to possess enough built-in redundancy to compensate for even seemingly catastrophic blows; abandoning the most direct pathway would not have worked for telephone grids, because the farther the message traveled through the network's wires and switches, and the more times its direction shifted, the more degraded the signal became. Digital messages, on the other hand, messages composed in the ones and zeros of computer object code, never degraded. They could bounce around indefinitely without losing their integrity, and still arrive pristine. There was another advantage to the digital approach. Since messages were broken down by the computer into long lists of ones and zeros, why not break them down into smaller bits, or "packets," and then reassemble them at the end point? That way even a message as simple as an email might take dozens of different pathways to its destination. It was more like teleportation than simple transmission: You disassembled the data into many distinct packets; cast them out on the network, where each packet found its own way; and then reassembled the data at the end point, all in microseconds, which are perceived by humans as real time. No delay. Diagrams of the proposed "packet-switching" network looked more like drawings of interlinked brain cells than a road map or a telephone grid. Such a network required minimal central planning, because each new computer node that connected just enlarged and strengthened the web. You could not destroy such a network easily, because even if you managed to take out a large chunk, traffic would automatically seek out surviving nodes.

This gave the Internet an especially hardy nature—a fact that buttressed the anarchic theology of the techno-utopians. But it was not invulnerable, as the massive 2002 DDoS attack demonstrated. The system's root servers were critical, because all Internet traffic relied on at least one of the thirteen. If you could mount a sufficiently powerful assault, it was theoretically possible to overwhelm all thirteen and bring even this very resilient global network to a dead stop. It would take a mighty computer to mount an attack like that, or one very, very large botnet. By the turn of the century, botnets were the coming thing . . .

. . . *and* they were getting easier to make.

In the beginning, networks were created by wiring computers together manually, but as the infrastructure of the Internet solidified, interconnection was a given. Almost all computers today are connected to a network, even if only to their local ISP. So if you were clever enough to make all the computers on a network work together, you could effectively assemble yourself a supercomputer. There was even a poorly guarded infrastructure already in place to facilitate such work. Techies had long been using Internet Relay Chat (IRC) channels to maintain constant real-time dialogue with colleagues all over the world. IRC offered a platform for global communication that was controlled from a single point, the channel's manager, and was used to host open-ended professional discussions, laboratory projects, and teleconferences before desktop applications for such things became widely known or available. Members of a group could use the channel to communicate directly and privately to one another but could also broadcast messages to the entire membership. Some of the earliest benign "bots" were crafted by IRC channel controllers to automatically monitor or manage discussion. The idea wasn't completely new. Computer operators had long written programs to automate routine tasks on their networks. These early bots were useful and harmless. In the late 1970s, a Massachusetts researcher named Bob Thomas created a silly worm he called "Creeper," which would display a message on infected machines: "I'm the Creeper, catch me if you can!" Creeper was more frog than worm. It hopscotched from target to target, removing itself from each computer as it jumped to the next. It was designed just to show off a little, and to make people laugh.

But even those engaged in noble pursuits sometimes don't play nice. Chat room members sometimes chose to commandeer these channels, to, in effect, become alternate controllers. One very effective way to hijack an IRC channel (to, in effect, create a botnet) was to bypass individual computer operators with a worm that could infect all the machines. The author seeded the network with his code and linked them to himself. The official manager of the channel would have no idea his network had been hijacked. The usurper could then marshal the power of the network to mount a DDoS attack against those with whom he disagreed or of whom he disapproved, or he could simply explore the network all he wished, collecting information from individual computers, spying, or issuing commands of his own. It was a tool ready-made for more nefarious purposes.

On Wednesday, November 4, 1988, as voters went to the polls nationwide to choose Vice President George H.

W. Bush over Governor Michael Dukakis of Massachusetts for the White House, a headline in the *New York Times* read:

"VIRUS" IN MILITARY COMPUTERS DISRUPTS SYSTEMS NATIONWIDE

The writer, John Markoff, reported:

In an intrusion that raises questions about the vulnerability of the nation's computers, a Department of Defense network has been disrupted since Wednesday by a rapidly spreading "virus" program apparently introduced by a computer science student.

. . . By late yesterday afternoon computer experts were calling the virus the largest assault ever on the nation's computers.

"The big issue is that a relatively benign software program can virtually bring our computing community to its knees and keep it there for some time," said Chuck Cole, deputy computer security manager at Lawrence Livermore Laboratory in Livermore, Calif., one of the sites affected by the intrusion. "The cost is going to be staggering."

For those inclined to conspiracy theories, it was noted with particular interest that the twenty-three-year-old author of the "virus," Robert Tappan Morris, a Cornell University graduate student, was the son of the chief scientist at the National Computer Security Center, a division of the National Security Agency. The younger Morris had grown up playing with computers. Typical of those in the hacking community, he had a fluency with networks and network security (such as it existed at that time, which is to say, nearly always not at all). By all accounts, he cooked up the worm on his own. Markoff reported that the grad student's creation had clogged computer networks nationwide; in 1988, these networks still mostly belonged to the military, corporations, and universities. Cliff Stoll, then working as a computer security expert at Harvard University, told the newspaper, "There is not one system manager who is not tearing his hair out. It is causing enormous headaches."

The managers were annoyed, certainly, but also clearly impressed. More than one programmer described the Morris Worm as "elegant." It consisted of only ninety-nine lines of code, and had a number of clever ways to invade computers, one of them by causing a *buffer overflow* (remember that technique?) in a file-sharing application of the ARPANET. Morris launched his worm from an IP address at Harvard University to cover his tracks at Cornell, expecting it to evade detection in the computers it infected. As smart as it was, the worm had a fatal flaw. In an effort to protect itself from being flushed out of a network, the code was designed to reproduce itself wantonly, and, much to Morris's dismay, ended up spiraling out of control. When he realized that it was running amok, he said he tried to send out instructions to kill it, but the networks were so jammed with his worm's traffic that the corrective could not get out.

Once it malfunctioned, Morris never tried to evade responsibility. He was later convicted under a new Federal Computer Fraud and Abuse Act, fined $10,000, and sentenced to three years of probation and four hundred hours of community service. Perhaps a more lasting punishment has been lifelong notoriety, a quasi-hero status among those who admire acts of cybervandalism. He is today an associate professor at MIT, and insists he had intended nothing more than to quietly infect computers in order to count them. Prosecutors charged that he had, in fact, designed the worm to "attack" computers owned by Sun Microsystems, Inc., and the Digital Equipment Corporation, two of the institutions hardest hit.

Prior to this stunning event, some in the tech field had differentiated between viruses and worms by classifying the former as malicious, the latter as beneficial. On purpose or not, Morris's worm confirmed its destructive potential. Geoffrey Goodfellow, president of Anterior Technology, Inc., told Markoff, "It was an accident waiting to happen. We deserved it. We needed something like this to bring us to our senses. We have not been paying too much attention to protecting ourselves." This kind of lament was becoming common . . . and we would hear it again.

As the Internet began to more fully congeal in the following decade, and as the personal computer became as commonplace in American homes as the TV set, malware preyed primarily on the explosive success of email. Having learned to invade computers and propagate over networks, malware creators were no longer content to demonstrate their ability to infect and spread; they were now intent on writing malware that could actually accomplish something. Making computers easy to use and linking them together had many wonderful effects, but it also created an ocean of suckers. Worms and viruses exploited the naïveté of new computer users, who readily fell victim to "Trojan horses," usually emails enticing them to open unsolicited attachments. One of the worst was the Melissa virus, so dubbed because its author, David L. Smith, admired a lap dancer by that name. It was inadvertently released from a sexually oriented website, and was designed initially to distribute pornographic images. It worked by attaching itself to a Microsoft Word document, and once downloaded by a single user, would raid email files for new targets and begin mass-mailing itself. Melissa rapidly clogged networks worldwide. Smith was arrested, served twenty months in prison, and was fined $5,000.

The email attachment technique is still used today, but peaked with the I Love You virus in 2000, which arrived as a mysterious email with a compelling come-on, "I Love You," and invited recipients to open the attached missive from an unknown admirer. It preyed on curiosity, loneliness, and vanity, and once invited into a computer, like

Melissa, sought out email files for new targets. This virus, designed by two programming students in the Philippines, was crafted to steal passwords from victims' personal files, but failed, so it fell more into the category of malicious mischief than theft. It resulted in an estimated $5.5 billion in damage, infecting as many as fifty million computers in a single day. Like the malware to come, it exploited a known vulnerability in Microsoft's operating system. It was the attack that prompted the software giant to get serious about protecting itself, and came, coincidentally, at precisely the time when Microsoft was hiring T. J. Campana. The success of these email virsuses made computer users more wary about opening unsolicited attachments, and helped create the lucrative antivirus industry.

Melissa and I Love You gave way to what Phil Porras calls "the Era of the Massive Worms." There would continue to be very successful email viruses, notably one named after tennis star Anna Kournikova, which took advantage of her fetching image to lure computer users into opening a "picture," but heightened security measures and pickier computer users gradually forced greater stealth.

Worms needed no human help. One of the first big ones was Code Red, which appeared on July 13, 2001, and was so called because the researchers who discovered it happened to be drinking a soda by that name. It created a buffer overflow in Windows Operating Systems by generating long strings of the letter N, thereby overflowing the buffer and hijacking the storing program. It defaced websites by displaying the triumphant message, "HELLO! Welcome to http://www.WORM.com! Hacked by Chinese!" It was soon so widespread that the phrase "Hacked by Chinese!"entered the language, appropriated by victorious online game players to lord it over defeated opponents. The author of Code Red was never caught, but most clues again pointed to the Philippines. It was thought to have infected 359,000 computers.

Code Red was followed by a succession of worms—Slammer, Blaster, Nimda, Sasser, and others—which increasingly focused on vulnerabilities Microsoft had already patched. But the Era of the Massive Worms effectively ended when the software giant released Service Pack 2 in 2004, buttoning up the operating system as never before. It marked the end of the naive early period of Internet development, which was defined by the happy notion that freely sharing all information would save the world. This belief still has its fierce adherents—WikiLeaks comes to mind—but the average computer user had learned his lesson by 2004. Microsoft, at least, had noticed snakes in the garden. Whereas Windows initially had been designed to have a strictly hospitable disposition, happily opening whatever packet of data came knocking, Service Pack 2 regarded anything inbound as a threat.

At the same time as the legitimate computer world was wising up, so was its evil counterpart. Malware in the first decade of the twenty-first century underwent something akin to the Cambrian Explosion, a period in evolutionary history when change seemed to accelerate. The key was the shift from malware as vandalism to malware for profit. Up until that point, those malfactors inept or unlucky enough to get caught were all what today's security experts call "script kiddies," amateurs who borrowed software written by others and attempted to employ it for their own ends. They had appropriated malware themselves that could spread, and make some sort of goofy display. But there remained a big stumbling block to actually using these rapid-spreaders to do something useful, specifically, to *make money.*

The next step was foreseeable. Profit is the universal trigger of innovation. At a malware conference in Washington, D.C., in October 2003, Stuart E. Schecter and Michael D. Smith, professors at Harvard's School of Engineering and Applied Sciences, noted that the opportunity was ripe for a "new class" of malware, one that they called an "access-for-sale worm."

"An access-for-sale worm . . . [enables] an individual to control a large number of systems and sell access to each one to the highest bidder," they wrote. "[It] enables the black hat community to work together to pool their skills and distribute risk in order to maximize the loot they extract," *loot* being money potentially drained from bank accounts, or valuable credit information. They predicted that the new worm would close the door through which it entered a system and repair the vulnerability "to prevent copycat worms from gaining access to the system." It would open a "back door" to invite privileged access to the botnet controller, and would report back information about the kind, value, and specific vulnerabilities of each system it invaded. Once such a botnet was created, control could be maintained with well-known public encryption methods. So long as the worm's creator restricted direct communication to an occasional update, he could set himself up as a middleman, providing the actual thief with a mechanism to steal while shielding himself from risk. Clients could select infected networks vulnerable to their specific criminal attempt, and even make test runs before renting the platform. Such an approach would combine the reach of a massive worm infection with the control of a small, targeted hack.

"Few of the worms released today are written for the financial benefit of the author," they wrote. "If the attacker wants to target a specific system, he will find it more effective to attack it directly or via a Trojan horse than to wait for a virus or a worm to propagate to it. If a worm's author attempts to trace the propagation of his creation through a network he risks detection through traffic analysis. Even if he can successfully track propagation he may not know the value of the systems he now had access to. These problems do not trouble the creator of an access-for-sale worm as he need not seek out the infected systems or know how to best profit from a targeted attack on them. Instead, he provides others with the ability to covertly detect whether machines are infected and offers to sell them the opportunity of gaining access to those systems. Along with the opportunity, the seller also transfers to the buyer the risks that come from such an intrusion."

And so it was. The enterprise migrated to organized crime and to nation-states. A new industry sprang up, primarily in Asia and Eastern Europe, a nemesis for the emerging computer security industry. This was not something even on the radar of the techno-utopians. For every antivirus company like Symantec there was now a "dark Symantec," a Bizarro World equivalent, bent on exploitation, filled with comparable experts and profitable enough to sustain research and development. Today there is big money for those who can stealthily invade computer networks, or construct a secure botnet, and no modern military arsenal is complete without state-of-the-art malware.

The worm credited, or blamed, for pushing the game from pranksterism to profit was Bagle, which appeared in 2004 as an email attachment and is still very much alive. It assembled about two hundred thousand computers into a botnet that still generates an estimated 5.7 billion spam messages daily. Bagle's innovation was to open a back door to Microsoft's Transmission Control Protocol, one of the most basic functions of the operating system that governs data exchange. A back door is a way of transferring data that avoids the computer's firewall by having the infected computer *invite* intrusion; it allows the botnet's controller to raid any data stored on the host. Bagle also blocked communication with antivirus sites, which prevented infected machines from being cleaned or updated, and it delivered in the text of the code a boastful poem for its enemies: "Greetz to antivirus companies

In a difficult world
In a nameless time
I want to survive
So you will be mine!!

It was even signed

Bagle Author
29.04.04
Germany.

Like a transitional species on the evolutionary tree, Bagle retained a certain hacker panache, but it also created a stable moneymaking platform. It could rapidly distribute advertisements for fake services or merchandise, raiding the contact lists on each of its bots to construct a branching tree of spam. The ads popped up on computer users' screens or in their mailboxes unsolicited, but from a known sender. While only a small percentage of increasingly wary computer users were fooled enough to send money, even a tiny percentage of 5.7 billion messages adds up to a substantial profit. In 2007, an email Trojan called Storm created a botnet easily three times larger than Bagle, and perhaps much larger than that. The "subject" line on incoming email tempted European users with information about a massive storm descending on the continent, hence the name Storm. Its author or authors have never been caught, have made self-protective adjustments over the years to combat the efforts of the white hats, and have managed to sustain a stable spam-generating monster. In the year after Storm came Torpig, a wickedly sophisticated Trojan that stole bank account and credit card information from an estimated half million computers.

The botnet was now a business model.

Once there was real money in it, new malware strains proliferated. There are scores of species in the digital taxonomy today. In parts of Eastern Europe and Asia, malware kits that enable script kiddies to put together exploits (like the one that presaged Conficker) are sold commercially in the same way that antivirus software is in the West, complete with customer assistance and regular updates to help customers keep up with the white hats' moves. Today's digitial viruses borrow from a bag of tricks perfected in the previous decade, and build on that foundation. Each strain that appears has its own specific antecedents. Conficker combined elements from two evolutionary pathways: worms and botnets.

Its worm characteristics stem from two of the most famous early examples: Sircam (2001) and Blaster (2003). Sircam arrived conventionally, attached to a missive with the subhead "Hi, how are you?" But then it did something new. It arrived as a Trojan horse but behaved as a worm once inside an operating system, using the host's data transfer applications to spread. The most obvious step Sircam took was to borrow a document from the host computer's files and forward it to another computer on the network. The incoming email would be from a familiar source, and would ask the recipient, "I send you this file in order to have your advice," or "I hope you like the file I send you," or use a variety of other awkwardly worded come-ons—English was clearly not its creators' first language. The files selected for forwarding were taken randomly from the computer's files, so they occasionally caused embarrassment, as private files were emailed to those who were never intended to see them. This feature caused most of the consternation about Sircam, but its most innovative contribution was something else.

The worm knew its way around Windows well enough to penetrate the core. It took control of the machine's file-sharing applications, and then replicated itself (in addition to activating the email scheme) by reaching directly into other computers on the network. This would be a central characteristic of Conficker.

Blaster was a purer strain of worm. Like Conficker, it was created by reverse-engineering a patch issued by Microsoft, and exploited a buffer overflow. Unlike its more cunning descendant, however, Blaster announced itself. Embedded in its code were two messages. One read, "LOVE YOU SAN!!" The other was a message for Bill Gates, reflecting the widespread resentment in the programming community of Microsoft's increasing domination of the software market. It read, "billy gates why do you make this possible? Stop making money and fix your software." It was also programmed to launch a massive DDoS attack on the company, but fizzled in part because it was aimed at the wrong company site and had to be redirected, giving Microsoft an opportunity to shut down the target. Still, Blaster caused an estimated $500 million in damages to computer networks worldwide. The most original feature of this worm was its ability to scan other computers on the host's network for those that would be vulnerable. This made its spread far more efficient, and would become one of the weapons in Conficker's arsenal.

Three early botnets likewise contributed innovations that Hassen Saidi found in Conficker. The Sinit Trojan of 2003 was not a particularly effective piece of malware, but it did introduce the use of encrypted communications with its command and control center. The use of encryption was telling. It revealed how competitive cybercrime had become and fulfulled Schecter's and Smith's prophecy. The designers of Sinit were trying to protect it not just from the white hats—there weren't that many security experts hunting them down at that point—but from rival criminals. The malware's code contained an IP address for the infected computer to call for instructions. Any black hat with that IP address could control the botnet. Any white hat could simply shut it down, or hijack it for further study. Counting the number of infected machines on botnets had become increasingly difficult. But if the white hats could take control, they could audit the network and make sure they shut down every infected machine. Sinit's encryption was the first effort to, in effect, fit the botnet with a lock. As we have seen, encryption was central to Conficker's strategy.

A Trojan called StartPage in 2005 posed only a minor threat, but introduced the tactic of checking to see what language was employed on the computer's keyboard.

The last and most significant innovation borrowed (and improved upon) by Conficker was first introduced in 2004 by a botnet called Bobax. It made a tactical advance on Sinit and other botnets. Bobax tried to hide its command center's location. By the mid-2000s, security experts could readily shut down botnets that communicated on an IRC channel. These had a single command and control center. If you found it, you could cut off the botnet's head, something the white hats were getting very good at. So the criminals devised a number of new strategies, among them the use of a domain name on the Internet instead of an IRC channel. Web traffic is very hard to shut down. Command centers became moving targets, shifting rapidly from one domain to another, hiding in the vast flood of Internet traffic.

Bobax generated a random list of domain names on a fixed schedule. This, as we will see, would turn out to be the most devilish feature of Conficker.

This tactic, hiding the botnet's controller behind a continually shifting list of Internet domain names, was also employed in June 2007 by a very successful Trojan horse dubbed Srizbi. Thought to have originated in Estonia, it invaded computers by posing as antivirus software. It spread rapidly throughout 2008, until it became one of the largest botnets ever, responsible at its height for three-quarters of the spam messages sent every day around the world. Researchers at a security firm called FireEye, working with others who would be central players in the effort to stop Conficker, were able to seize control of the botnet briefly by using its domain name-generating algorithm to spit out lists of all its future contact points, buying them up, and shutting them down. They had the botnet nearly completely contained in 2008 until they missed one of the domain names, which was all it took for Srizbi's creator to regain control. Srizbi suffered a deep setback later that year, however, shortly before Conficker appeared, when federal authorities raided a notorious California ISP that had been serving as its host.

So when Conficker debuted on November 20, 2008, it stood on the shoulders of two decades of research and development, trial and error. It was as much a product of evolution as anything in nature. Instead of being assembled by genes, the worm was assembled by "memes," a word coined by British scientist and polemicist Richard Dawkins in his 1976 book, *The Selfish Gene*. Memes are original ideas. Dawkins argued that they play the same role in cultural evolution as genes play in biology, getting passed along from person to person, surviving and adapting as they move.

But there was a parallel evolution going on. Just as there were villains who used their deeper knowledge to make a living from the ignorance of others, there were heroes, too, geeks who stood up for the Internet's integrity, and who used their skills to do good, not evil.

The white hats in this struggle were locked in the old and eternal battle of good vs. evil, God vs. Satan.

Game on.

5

THE X-MEN

HE AND OTHERS LIKE HIM, BORN WITH GENETIC
POTENTIAL FOR GREAT POWERS, ARE KNOWN AS
MUTANTS. THE WORLD OF HUMANS FEARS THEM
FOR BEING DIFFERENT . . . AND HATES THEM FOR
BEING GIFTED.

—The X-Men Chronicles

By mid-December, three weeks after Conficker first appeared, the worm had burrowed into well over a million computers worldwide. It had spread silently for six days before it began regularly trying to connect with its botmaster, who could have been hiding behind any of the 250 domain names the worm generated afresh each day. Such a large infection became a noisy presence on the Internet.

Yet still it had attracted no attention outside the Tribe. A select but widely scattered circle of computer security experts watched with mounting concern, mindful of what a botnet of that size could do. Beyond this group, word of a new and major botnet surfaced only at the website

Ars Technica, a technology journal owned by Condé Nast with a very small readership. An article by Joel Hruska on December 2 called Conficker "a rising specter," but the story was upbeat, suggesting that the various private security firms and academics monitoring it had the threat under control.

Like many of those in the field, Hruska took Conficker at face value. Since its only known use was a simple moneymaking scheme—to download the fraudware package at *TrafficConverter.biz* that had given the worm its name—he portrayed the worm as pedestrian. His post focused on the fact that it had spread even though, or more likely *because,* Microsoft had patched the vulnerability it exploited—the buffer overflow opportunity at Port 445.

"Microsoft appears to have dealt with the problem in a textbook fashion," Hruska wrote. ". . . It would be extremely fascinating to see data on how a patch spreads throughout the Internet once released. . . . Events like this raise the question of whether or not Microsoft should have the capability to push critical security updates out to home users automatically, regardless of how AutoUpdate is configured. . . . How do you solve a security problem that's caused by users refusing to update their machines?"

While the new worm was raising some interesting questions, it was not yet in the same league as Storm or Srizbi. As he saw it, the big commercial security firms like Symantec, F-Secure, I-Defense and others were dissecting it and figuring out how to contain it, with an eye toward offering remedial software for sale somewhere down the line.

The problem was already known to be bigger than that in the security community, but since there is no such thing as an agency charged with protecting the Internet for its own sake, concern about Conficker proceeded from a variety of narrower motives. The AV industry was worried about protecting its customers, but was also mindful that the growing lists of bots represented a potential gold mine of new customers—since the malware disabled security updates, each bot was a prime mark for remedial software (the botnet itself was a valuable list of *unprotected* computers). The telecoms folks were interested in protecting their vital networks from DDoS attacks. Microsoft wanted to safeguard its customers and reputation, while researchers like Phil Porras at SRI had more of a purely academic interest, figuring out what this latest wrinkle from the black hats meant.

That was the focus in Menlo Park. The work demanded aptitude, but also years of experience. It has been almost thirty years since computers became ubiquitous, and twenty since the Internet blinked to life, so the youngsters who were the first to embrace networks and operating systems are now middle-aged. The elders of the Tribe remember the old Altair 8080 kits, but most of its elite übergeeks today were the first generation to grow up with computers, and have absorbed an intuitive fluency with networks. Today they work for software companies, research labs, security firms, telecommunications companies, government, or Internet service organizations. Whatever the overarching agendas of their employers, these guys (and they were mostly men) were viscerally drawn to fighting Conficker. This was intellectual combat, pitting the best good-guy minds against the best bad-guy minds.

The dozen or so white hats who joined this fight, which would eventually include Phil Porras, the man who best understood the worm, assembled in the orbit of T. J. Campana, who wielded Microsoft's deep pockets and clout. Among them were Rick Wesson, a brash forty-two-year-old San Francisco entrepreneur who was CEO of his own Internet security firm, coauthor of some central Internet protocols, and owner of his own small Internet registrar; Rodney Joffe, the eldest member at fifty-five and a self-proclaimed "adult in the room," a burly transplanted South African from Phoenix who was (among other things) security chief of Neustar, a telecommunications company that operated the *.biz* top-level domain and several Internet registries; Andre DiMino, a quiet, self-possessed New Jerseyite who worked for Bergen County law enforcement during the day, but by night was one of the founders of a unique nonprofit botnet-killing service called Shadowserver. Joining them were Paul Vixie, a dour and irascible geek who is one of the architects of the Internet and who was on the board of trustees of the American Registry for Internet Numbers; Andre "Dre"

Ludwig, the youngest member at age twenty-eight, a self-taught computer security consultant in Alexandria, Virginia, with a big reputation and a forthright, confrontational style; John Crain, a transplanted Brit who lived in Long Beach, traveled the world for ICANN (the global nonproft agency that assigns domain names and IP addresses), and had a penchant for cowboy attire; and Chris Lee, a meticulous graduate student at Georgia Tech who would end up running the bulk of the sinkholing operation.

To varying degrees, as individuals, they had warned in speeches and articles about the ludicrous fragility of the Internet, as the global net grew and grew, and as society kept leaning on it more and more heavily. They were accustomed to being ignored. Some took it better than others, and remained hopeful. Some were more fatalistic, assuming that at some point the whole thing was going to crash. In their darkest moods, some of them—Vixie and Wesson come to mind—could be positively surly about it, like the engineer who tries to explain for the thousandth time that luck does not lessen risk, even when it seems to—*You do realize, Mr. NASA Chief Engineer, that just because you keep getting away with these Space Shuttle launches, it doesn't mean that sucker is any less likely to blow up on national TV.*

In the case of the Internet, and those who understood it best, you could sense beneath the immediate concern a deeper frustration, the exasperation of someone who has spent every minute, every hour, every day of his life feeling smarter than everyone else, only to be dismissed as strange. Paul Vixie had a lecture called "Vixie's Internet Rant," which details the train of errors committed by the architects of the Internet, who designed it to be shared by like-minded, friendly colleagues, without a thought to what might happen when a billion strangers crashed the party.

At the 2005 DefCon 13 Convention, an annual hackers' gathering, one of the few places in the world where geeks do not encounter the Glaze, here is Paul delivering his rant: a thickly built man in a black Spamarama T-shirt with a broad clean-shaven face, big glasses, crew-cut black hair, and heavy, dark eyebrows. He is speaking in a low, affectless monotone, his hands held stiffly at his sides. His speech is highly technical, weirdly more powerful for its peculiar delivery, and, if you are paying close attention, darkly humorous. It frames the annals of global interconnection as a perfect instance of historical folly, meeting all the criteria set down by the historian Barbara Tuchman in her book *The March of Folly*: it was the action of a group, not an individual; it consistently chose the "boneheaded" course over others that were obviously correct; and the chosen course was not just something discovered to be mistaken in retrospect, but something *known to be stupid* in its own time. Paul encouraged audience members to pick up the book, and offered to personally refund the purchase price if they did not find it alarmingly pertinent.

"What were they thinking?" Vixie asked. "*Were* they thinking?"

Government took it on the chin in this presentation, for its lack of foresight and of oversight, for its inability to see the danger—and Paul would be the first to tell you that things haven't changed. Indeed, as we will see, the government was notably absent from the effort against Conficker.

It is one of the peculiarities of modern times that as industrialized nations depend more and more on computer networks for everything, relatively little thought has been given to protecting them. The United States spends billions on its military, not just to protect its own borders, but to project force anywhere in the world on short notice. Yet the telecommunications networks that increasingly undergird every aspect of modern life, not to mention the military itself, are shockingly vulnerable to infiltration and sabotage, not just from pranksters and cybercriminals, but from the very nations the United States are most likely to confront as enemies.

"Private sector networks in the United States, networks operated by civilian U.S. government agencies, and unclassified U.S. military and intelligence agency networks increasingly are experiencing cyber intrusions and attacks," said a U.S.-China Economic and Security Review Commission report to Congress that was published the same month Conficker appeared. ". . . Networks connected to the Internet are vulnerable even if protected with hardware and software firewalls and other security mechanisms. The government, military, businesses and economic institutions, key infrastructure elements, and the population at large of the United States are completely dependent on the Internet. Internet-connected networks operate the national electric grid and distribution systems for fuel. Municipal water treatment and waste treatment facilities are controlled through such systems. Other critical networks include the air traffic control system, the system linking the nation's financial institutions, and the payment systems for Social Security and other government assistance on which many individuals and the overall economy depend. *A successful attack on these Internet-connected networks could paralyze the United States* [emphasis added]."

The ad hoc group that formed to combat Conficker reached out repeatedly to government agencies, including law enforcement, the military, the intelligence community, and every other agency you might expect to have an interest in protecting the computer networks of the nation (not to mention . . . *the world*). They eventually succeeded in getting reps from the alphabet soup—NSA, DOD, CIA, FBI, DHS, etc.,—to sign on as members of the private chat channel where they coordinated strategy, but throughout the effort the feds would remain lurkers; they logged in and listened, but rarely made a peep. Over four months in December 2008 and January, February, and March 2009, as Conficker assembled the largest botnet in the world, government, which would seem to have had the largest share of overarching responsibility, played a shockingly minor role. At first the übergeeks assumed the feds were constrained by the need for secrecy: you know, protecting official tactics and methods. Surely behind the scenes there was a sophisticated, well-funded clandestine *official* apparatus—everyone has seen the gleaming, dark glass and metal, see-everything/hear-everything sets Hollywood dusts off for its espionage blockbusters. What the anti-Conficker group discovered was deeply disillusioning. The real reason for the feds' silence was . . . *they had nothing to offer!* They were in way over their heads.

So the battle was in the hands of this odd and uniquely talented collection of volunteers. Given the esoteric nature of the combat, it lent itself less to the analogies of earthbound warfare than to the fantastic. It called to mind DC Comics' "Justice League of America," or, better still, "X-Men," because this was definitely more of a Marvel crowd. What were superheroes, after all, but those with special powers? Marvel's creations were also invariably outsiders, not just special but *mutant,* a little bit off, defiantly antisocial, prone to sarcasm and cracking wise, suspicious of authority, both governmental and corporate (as T.J., Mr. Microsoft, would learn, to his chagrin). There is not one of the übergeeks involved who had not, at one time or another in his life, realized that he could run rings around the safeguards and defenses of most computer systems. The X-Men could make things happen that others could not. Knowledge empowered them: Rick Wesson commandeering the engineering computer system at Auburn as an undergrad to generate supercool fractal-based images, which he then copied on T-shirts and sold; T.J. providing free movies and music to his friends at FSU; another, who still wishes to go unnamed, who disassembled the mechanism for commercial online gaming so that he could play for free. This facility for computers and networks, being able to puzzle through the defenses of powerful systems, was very much like possessing a superpower—LADIES AND GENTLEMEN, THE TRUTH IS THAT MUTANTS ARE VERY REAL, AND THAT THEY ARE **AMONG** US. Even the standard cerebral, geeky civilian alter ego stereotype applied, since few of these guys were the least bit intimidating or commanding in person. They went about their day jobs as unassuming techies, men whose conversation was guaranteed to produce the Glaze, but out here in the cyberworld they were nothing less than the Anointed, the Guardians, the Special Ones: not just the ones capable of *seeing* the threat that no one else could see, but the only ones who could conceivably stop it—"We are the last line of defense at this point. . . . There are no others," T.J. wrote to the group early on. "You all are the smartest people in the security industry. . . . If not us . . . who? If not now . . . when?"

They were psyched!

But we are getting ahead of ourselves . . .

In mid-December 2008, the chat channel was up, a private Listserv—the List!—where these real-life X-Men, Rick Wesson, Rodney Joffe, Andre DiMino, and the others, plotted strategy, shared insights, coordinated efforts, and kept up a running dialogue. Anything posted to the List was available to the entire group, and most of it dealt with the minutiae of technical analysis, code-breaking, sinkholing, etc. Much of it read like this:

```
MD5: 38c3d2efdd47b1034b1624490ce1f3f2
>> SHA1: c6c1ed21ea15c8648a985dbabc8341cf1e3aa21e
>
>> That's the unpacked version and it was sent by
VirusTotal on Monday.
```

Or like this:

```
> <<ip, port, Host, time, getstring, referer, useragent, p0f>>
A fixed src port and linux p0f; dozens of GETs in under 3
seconds . . . this suggests a likely script. Others have noted a
python
2.6 urllib user-agent:
```

But from time to time various members would use the List as a soapbox or sounding board, speculating, proposing, arguing, praising, lamenting, criticizing, sometimes with real eloquence. Mining these exchanges and ventings reveals a detailed chronicle of the effort, often minute by minute. So the history of this remarkable technological drama, which might be called the First Internet World War, and which took place almost entirely out of the public eye, unfolds as a series of missives, like an epistolary novel. Shades of Samuel Richardson!

As the threat mounted, working with the X-Men became a mark of status. Here was a band of warriors for the Internet, which is to say warriors for civilization. It sounds corny, but it was true. Most of the core members knew one another well: Paul Vixie wrote in one of his first postings to the List, "Whenever I'm added to a security list, I look around for [the usual suspects] and a bunch of other regulars, and if they're not there yet I know they'll be along in a few weeks. Sometimes I even nominate them myself just to cut down on the suspense." Those who wished to join had to be vouched for by others already on the List, and some were turned away: "I feel like we are in high school," wrote Rick Wesson. But there were only a few hundred people in the world capable of the work.

By the end of December, the X-Men were regularly pulling all-nighters, trying to stay one step ahead of the evil botmaster. T.J. was working until ten o'clock most nights in his office up in one of Microsoft's Redmond sprockets. His boss would stop by, surprised to see him in so late.

"What are you doing?" he'd ask.

"Conficker."

"Everything okay?"

"Well, the Internet's melting. We're just keeping it from melting completely."

The bad guys behind Conficker, its unknown botmaster, would prove to be worthy adversaries. They were villains in the truest sense, talented programmers bent on using their powers for evil. And the world war was about nothing less than the soul of the future, *the soul of the new global mind.* As for as the X-Men, what could be cooler than to be right in the middle of it, showing off your chops?

6

DIGITAL DETECTIVES

THIS MAY NOT BE MUCH OF A WORLD . . . MAY
NOT EVEN BE THE WORLD IT IS SUPPOSED TO
BE . . . BUT IT IS OUR WORLD NEVERTHELESS.
AND WE WILL FIGHT FOR IT.
—The Amazing X-Men

At the October 2008 botnet conference in Arlington, Virginia, the one where T. J. Campana unveiled Microsoft's "out of band" emergency patch, he had handed a sheet of paper to Andre DiMino.

"Do you know anything about this?" he asked.

It was a printout of information about Gimmiv, the first piece of malware that used the Chinese kit to exploit the newly discovered Port 445 vulnerability. Andre didn't recognize the strain offhand, but he was the right person to ask.

On a Monday morning ten years earlier, Andre had stumbled into the malware wars when he discovered that over the weekend someone had broken into the computer system he was managing for a small company in New Jersey. Andre has an undergraduate degree in electrical engineering with an emphasis in computer science, but most of what he knows about botnets he has taught himself. At forty-five, he is a tall, slender man whose dark hair is cropped close to his scalp. He is affable and quietly idealistic, and he has a selfless passion for his work. His day job is doing computer forensics for the Bergen County prosecutor, but the work that drives him most is done before a small array of computers in an upstairs bedroom of his suburban New Jersey home.

Andre has a sense of mission, of higher purpose. He hunts bad guys in cyberspace for free. His email arrives with a New Testament admonition, from Saint Paul's first letter to the Thessalonians: "Make sure that nobody pays back wrong for wrong, but always try to be kind to each other and to everyone else." He has a very particular code of ethics about his work, which makes him something like a photographic negative of those he combats, and a rarity even among those fighting the good fight. A whole industry has grown up around protecting vulnerable computer networks for profit. Andre is determined *not* to profit from his work; once he hunts down a compromised computer network he informs the owner of the problem free of charge . . . just because it is *the right thing to do*. Then he kills the botnet.

Back when he discovered that weekend break-in at his old employer's offices, Andre assumed it was the work of a hacker, a vandal, or possibly a disgruntled former employee, only to discover, from an analysis of the IP addresses of the incoming data, that the company's network had been invaded by someone from Turkey or Ukraine. What would someone halfway around the planet want with the computer network of a small business-management firm in a New Jersey office park? Apparently, judging by what he found, his invader was in the business of selling pirated software, movies, and music. Just as T.J. Campana had discovered at FSU, the pirates had gone looking for large amounts of digital storage space in which to hide stolen inventory. They appeared to have conducted an automated search over the Internet, looking worldwide for vulnerable systems with large amounts of unused disc space—Andre compares it to walking around rattling doorknobs, looking for one door left unlocked. His network fit the bill, so the crooks had dumped a huge bloc of data onto his discs. He erased the stash and locked the door that had allowed the pirates in. As far as Andre's employer was concerned, that solved the problem. No harm done. No need to call the police or investigate further.

But Andre was intrigued. He reviewed the server logs for previous weeks and saw that this successful invasion was one of many such efforts. Other attackers had been rattling the doors of his network, looking for vulnerabilities. If there were bad guys actively exploiting other people's computers all over the world, designing sophisticated programs to exploit weaknesses . . . how cool was that? And who was trying to stop them?

He set about educating himself on the fine points of this obscure battle. He eventually founded, along with a like-minded botnet hunter named Nicholas Albright, The Shadowserver Foundation, a nonprofit partnership of defense-minded geeks at war against malware, effectively transforming himself into a digital Sam Spade—indeed, the graphic atop Shadowserver's home page features a Dashiell Hammett–style detective emerging from shadow. Today the organization coordinates the donated labor of like-minded cybervigilantes all over the world, tracking and, whenever possible, killing botnets. With the help of scores of volunteers and automated software like the program that monitors Phil Porras's net at SRI, they snare and catalog every new strain of malware that appears. Then they dissect it and trace it back to its source, all the while monitoring it to chart its activity and reach. This is time-consuming, sometimes tedious work, and apart from the satisfaction of slaying Internet dragons, there are few rewards.

In the beginning, Andre was rarely even thanked. At first Shadowserver's discoveries and notices were more likely to be met by disbelief and suspicion. Shadowserver would spot a new botnet taking shape and track the flow of data back to a particular network, and then to a specific IP address on that network, and then notify the service provider of the problem.

"This is not an attack from the outside," Andre would tell the ISP's security chief, who may or may not have noticed an uptick in traffic on his network. "This is something from the inside."

More often than not, the information was received grudgingly. Here was someone unknown—"They probably thought we were just a bunch of garage hackers," says Andre, "calling to tell the professional that his network had a flaw. They tended to react defensively." The fact that some amateur ninja had been sniffing around their network didn't go over too well, either. Most security managers were conditioned to treat such people as the *threat*, not realizing that the problem had outgrown the hacker stage. Either that or the IT manager just felt Andre was some smart-ass trying to show him up. The idea that there was selfless hacker offering managers useful information about their own network, for *free*, was hard to believe.

Brian Krebs, then one of just a handful of newspaper reporters (he was working for the *Washington Post* at the time) covering computer security, was so impressed that he wrote a cover story for the paper's Sunday magazine about Shadowserver.

Botnets were becoming a big problem, and Krebs thought the work Andre and Nick were doing was very much needed. He was surprised to find that there were these guys doing what he had hoped *someone* was doing. The industry was full of sellouts; people with a good idea would approach a big company with it and cash in. Here were a group of guys doing this work, which not many people even know how to do, infiltrating and cataloging botnets, and doing it as a public service. Krebs himself found it hard to believe.

In the 2006 article, "Bringing Botnets Out of the Shadows," Krebs wrote: "Botnets are the workhorses of most online criminal enterprise today, allowing hackers to ply their trade anonymously—sending spam, sowing infected PCs with adware from companies that pay for each installation, or hosting fraudulent e-commerce and banking sites. . . . Constant attack and setbacks can take an emotional toll on volunteers who spend countless hours not only hunting down bot herders but in many cases notifying the individuals or institutions whose networks and systems the hackers have commandeered. This is largely a thankless job, because in most cases the victims never even respond."

Gratitude started to come once Kreb's article put Shadowserver on the map. The cause brought like-minded geeks out of the woodwork, and the organization grew. It started getting requests for information from the FBI and Secret Service. Some consideration was given at that point to taking Shadowserver commercial. The data the foundation collected were undeniably valuable: this information clued large servers and networks in to looming threats and cataloged vulnerable systems. Charging would at least enable Shadowserver to pay people for their time, effort, and talent. But the group decided to keep doing the work for free. Andre saw it this way: *If you knew someone's house was in danger of catching on fire, would you simply warn him or offer to sell him the information?* By early 2009, the group had a ten-member core, and lots of carefully screened volunteers. Andre wanted to do the work full-time, and fantasized about a large grant or sponsorship that would enable him and the other core members to do so, but they all still needed their day jobs. They were collecting thousands of malware strains, snaring as many as ten thousand samples in their honeypots every day. Shadowserver played a central role in battling botnets, and received thousands of requests daily from network managers for technical reports.

With that many strains to track, Andre didn't recognize Gimmiv right away when T.J. approached him at the October conference. He checked his records. The Chinese exploit didn't amount to much, but he could see Microsoft's concerns. With an exploit kit available for a fee, and with MS08-067 advertising the vulnerability, he could see just as Microsoft did that something worse was probably on its way.

There is no formal relationship between the various computer security companies, labs, or organizations, so Conficker's arrival in late 2008 was noted and assessed by each in its own way. Eventually Hassen Saidi's reverse-engineering of the worm out in Menlo Park would prove to be the most definitive, but dozens of other experts were trying. Conficker was too big to ignore. Andre also took notice of it right away, not because he connected it immediately with Gimmiv, but because of its rapid and remarkable success. Within days, Shadowserver's honeypots all over the world were filling up with it the same way Phil Porras's was at SRI. Andre was alarmed. He learned from a colleague working for F-Secure in Finland that the worm was using a domain-name-generating tactic similar to Srizbi's.

So he had begun tracking it. Andre was accustomed to seeing botnets with a few hundred thousand drones. As this one reached a million, then two million, then three, then four, it felt scary. Its potential to do harm grew with its size. Nobody was more accustomed to dealing with botnets than he was, but the scale of this one was daunting. It was clearly more than your average spambot. What if this was the work of a nation-state? What was it for? How did you begin to stop it?

No one was deeper into those questions than Phil. He and his team had already seen that the initial fraudware scam, the effort to download fake antivirus software from the now defunct *TrafficConverter.biz*, was not the ultimate purpose of this botnet. They had come to believe that Conficker was unlike anything they had seen before. It was not some quick moneymaking scheme. It was not an effort to show off. The worm itself carried no specifically harmful payload. It had bigger ambitions. It was quietly and effectively building an infrastructure, a sturdy platform for malicious activity.

It was a tool, one that could be used to launch whatever its controller wanted, from a simple spam operation to an all-out attack on the world's digital vitals. And it was hard to believe that anyone with the ability to create such a tool would not have big ambitions for it.

At heart, the Internet is a protocol, a carefully choreographed method of moving data from one computer to another. The specific protocol that defines it, that makes it possible, is Transmission Control Protocol/Internet Protocol (TCP/IP), a suite of programs for sharing data created by the U.S. Defense Department when Richard Nixon was president. In order to move data from one machine to another, you have to know what is being sent, and how it is going to look at the other end of the transaction. Protocol, a word borrowed from diplomacy, defines how to package and send data so that it can be recognized and processed between computers. Home users are usually customers of an ISP, which enables them to connect with the Internet. It assigns each machine on its network an IP address, and usually has a different set of IP addresses with which it identifies those machines to the world. Every packet of data sent from a computer is given a header, which is essentially the same information as that on the outside of an envelope in traditional mail—the home address and the destination address. The ISP ships this packet to a router, a large computer that governs traffic flow.

Conceptually speaking, the Internet has three layers. Layer One consists of the actual Network Interface Cards

(NICs), the extensions inside computers that enable it to link with a network, and cables. Layer Two is made up of routers and switches, the subnet of computers that direct traffic, and the software that breaks Internet messages into packets. Governance of this layer was primarily in the hands of the Internet Assigned Numbers Authority. The American Registry for Internet Numbers (ARIN) is responsible for keeping track of IP addresses in the United States, Canada, and parts of the Caribbean. Layer Three consists of "applications," the domains created by organizations or individuals to be their public face in cyberspace. This was the layer overseen by ICANN, which is primarily responsible for the domain name registries, which authorize the registrars who actually serve customers who purchase domain names. Most malware attacked this upper level, Layer Three. Conficker utilized Layer Two, using the IP address system to set up an ever-shifting command center.

Blocking access to that command center was the immediate challenge. Hassen Saidi had grafted the worm's domain generating algorithm to his own clock in the lab. When he set the clock forward, the worm would dutifully spit out the list of 250 prospective domain names for that future date. To get out ahead of the worm, the X-Men would have to register all 250 of those domains in advance. If they succeeded, then the worm's creator would have no way to communicate with the botnet. Checkmate.

The side benefit, once you controlled all of the places

contacted by the botnet from day to day, was to own a running tally of infected, vulnerable computers. As that list grew each day, it gained in value. Whoever owned it would possess the most precious feature of the botnet. To actually seize control would require breaking the worm's code, but the list itself could be sold or leased to web scammers, thieves, or even nation-states. And any botnet the size of Conficker would contain some particularly valuable networks, those owned by corporations, banks, or government agencies.

Phil needed someone more familiar with the whole domain name system than he was, but also someone he could trust. He approached Rick Wesson, who had worked with him before, and who lived right in the San Francisco Bay area. Rick owned, among other things, a small domain name registrar. Indeed, Rick had been among the first people in the world to even know what one was.

He was part of the Internet's first wave of cocky young entrepreneurs, one of the many young geeks who moved to California twenty years ago to catch the coming digital wave. He dressed informally; a short man with an often messy, close-cropped head of reddish brown hair, he had, despite his forty-some years, the looks and manner of a college student. He favored T-shirts and jeans and despite his accomplishments and success still clung to an undergrad sensibility—for example, telling an audience at a 2007 symposium where he was invited to speak that he was "hungover," so he planned to keep his presentation "light." He spoke in a high-pitched, soft, singsong that disguised his natural bluntness and irreverence, and somehow made them more startling. This soothing tone was absent from his written messages, which could be jarring—"I'm not going to stop telling you what I think," he wrote to one offended colleague, "Get used to it." Rick was largely self-taught, and since personal computers were still relatively new, there were few elders around who could match his expertise. He had first used his hacking skills in Florida to print fake report cards for himself and his friends, which got him kicked out of high school. So he landed a computer security job while completing the course work to get admitted to Auburn University. It was there, as a freshman in the late 1980s, that he started his first business selling T-shirts decorated with cool fractal images he generated with the university's engineering school computers.

Rick had hippie leanings, but about two decades too late. He graduated from Auburn in 1992 and took a job teaching at Summit High School in Breckenridge, Colorado, where the principal was planning to float a bond issue to fund a computer network to connect all of the district's schools and libraries. Rick got excited about the project—he had actually written a book while still a student at Auburn about computer networking. The principal had a friend with IBM, and together they envisioned a closed computer network that the big computer company would install and manage.

Rick saw the project as a boondoggle. See, there was this amazing new tool called the Internet that offered to same connectivity . . . *for free*. Building the network would still have costs, but only a small fraction of IBM's proposal. It was a no-brainer. Except, of course, that when Rick tried to explain, the principal said no. A little too preemptively, in Rick's estimation. There was a scene. Rick might have thrown some binders around the principal's office. It led to his resignation.

So instead of steering the Breckenridge, Colorado, school system into the Internet vanguard, Rick worked for a few months washing dishes at a ski resort, and then he and his girlfriend, Pilar, got a bus, which they called the "Green Tortoise," and—shades of Ken Kesey and the Merry Pranksters—loaded it with pot and few dozen friends, and pointed it south, touring and smoking and drinking, all the way to Guatemala—Rick was more of a beer man himself, but fitted right in with the potheads. His wanderings next took him to Europe, through Spain, to Paris, and eventually to Turkey, where Rick met a German who was determined to set up the first Internet domain name registry in his country. The Internet was taking off, and it was clear that domain names were going to be the primary sorting mechanism for it. He followed the fellow to Düsseldorf, where they set up the business, and then Rick decided that the United States was ripe for the same kind of project.

Before most people had ever heard of the Internet, Rick

recognized it as an opportunity. The world was going to become a more efficient place, with detailed expert advice on every conceivable subject right at your fingertips! Answers to difficult problems waiting to be downloaded for free! When he was a senior at Auburn, a professor had sent him with a group of other students to a local office supply company, in an exercise to design a computer-based solution to an actual workplace problem. The issue presented to Rick's team was tracking inventory. The other members consulted with the company about the problem, and wrote a program themselves that ultimately didn't work. Rick was not wired to play well with others, and, besides, he had a better idea than his teammates. Why write a bad program when you could borrow one that worked well? He tapped into the nascent Internet and found some free inventory-tracking software that worked like a charm. He downloaded it and implemented it successfully at the local company. The company was happy. Problem solved! His professor flunked him, explaining to Rick that the essence of the assignment had been to cooperate to design an original solution. He could see his teacher's point, but it irked him. *Come on!* Why waste your time trying to invent something that had already been invented? The real problem, as Rick saw it, was the same one that would lose him the teaching job in Breckenridge. These guys had never heard of the Internet! The failing grade had left him several credits shy of graduation, and set him back a full semester.

He returned from Düsseldorf in the mid-1990s with a clear business model in his head. He landed an IT job in Silicon Valley, and the owners helped him set up a consulting business and signed on as his first client. In the ensuing years he started and sold a string of businesses. Pilar joined the organic food boom, and they moved out to a farm. Rick's work led him to some early work on Internet governance and technology. He was involved in writing some of the early protocols for ICANN, and as a result knew the workings of that system like the back of his hand.

The Internet, unlike roads, pipelines, or electrical grids, is not organized along physical pathways. Given the packet-switching method it employs to move data, more teleportation than straight transmission, there are no clearly defined pathways for its unceasing traffic. It is organized more like a phone book than a road map. The keys to routing packets were "identifiers," the domain names given to specific locations. There are nearly two hundred million domain names registered. The names are sold, cataloged, and maintained by commercial registrars, which are governed by registries. The registries themselves are overseen by ICANN, which functions as the primary phone book, the job it took over from SRI in 1998. At the low end of this system is the local ISP, which provides routing services for computers linked to its network, whether home users who buy a connection from a commercial provider or an office computer linked to an in-house network with its own server. These millions of small servers are grouped under three hundred or so Top Level Domains, signified by the letters that come after the period at the end of an email or web address—*.com, .biz, .edu, .de,* etc. If your email address ends with *Loyola.edu,* then Loyola (Loyola University) is your local domain, and *.edu* is your Top Level Domain, the designation for universities.

So domain names are the postal addresses of cyberspace. Each individual computer has its own address, which is assigned to it by its ISP. In order to connect with a website on the Internet, your computer sends the address to its ISP. To make things easier for human users, that address, which consists of a long line of numbers and symbols in computer language, is translated into a recognizable word—e.g., *www.google.com,* or *harvard.edu.* Keeping track of all of these millions of names is an industry made up of thousands of small registrars. Each registrar operates a server, which makes sure there are no duplicate names, and which can route messages to that domain.

At a time when few people outside Silicon Valley had ever heard of such things, Rick used the experience in Düsseldorf to form his own registrar. He named it *ar.com,* short for "Alice's Registry," after the famous talking blues performance by Arlo Guthrie, and obtained a license from ICANN to sell domain names. Ten years later, Rick was regarded as a pioneer. In 2002, he was appointed to ICANN's committee on security.

Security issues had begun to intrigue him primarily as an intellectual challenge. He saw the threat posed by botnets, and that few even in the IT business knew how to stop them. Not just stop them but how to track and monitor them. When he joined ICANN's security committee, he learned that the agency did not even knew how many botnets there were. Nobody was paying attention. So he formed a new company called Support Intelligence, and set about filling the need. He used the large Internet interface afforded by *ar.com* to assemble honeynets, and begin compiling research data. If he could measure them and capture their traffic, he could identify which computer networks—academic, corporate, government—were *pwned*. Then he could sell that information—he did not share Andre's compunction about profit. Rick had, partly by design but largely by happenstance, maneuvered his way into the leading edge of Internet security.

So when Phil was looking for somebody who would know how to tie up in advance all 250 of the domain names Conficker would generate daily, he thought of Rick, who had become a well-known player in Internet governance circles. Rick knew all about the new worm, of course. When Phil contacted him on December 15, it had already been spreading for three weeks. There were known infections in 106 countries. It was the talk of the computer security world.

"We've fully recovered the Conficker assembly and have been plowing through it in detail," Phil emailed him.

"We've cracked the domain generating algorithm and have a full listing of domains that will be generated for the next 200 days."

Phil started supplying Rick with daily lists of domains, and Rick used his contacts in the Internet governance community to purchase them. He then rented S3 storage space from Amazon to park the domains and "sinkhole" the millions of requests that poured in each day. The requests were simply routed to a dead-end location.

At the same time, Phil emailed the U.S. Computer Emergency Readiness Team (U.S. CERT), the agency responsible for protecting government computer networks, suggesting that it begin doing the same. That way the agency could scan all of the infected IP addresses and find out whether any government systems had been invaded, particularly whether any Defense Department networks had been breached. He received a return email thanking him for the suggestion.

Setting aside 250 domains a day was a big task, but not overwhelming. Rick stayed busy registering sites, and compiling sinkholing data on his Amazon account. He began pulling others into the effort, or connecting with others who were already at work on it, and started the List to coordinate their efforts. Georgia Tech grad student Chris Lee eventually offered his laboratory network as a home for the growing sinkhole, and some of the incoming botnet traffic began accumulating there. Andre was also sinkholing some with Shadowserver, and charting the botnet's growth.

By the end of December, Conficker had infected 1.5 million computers in 195 countries. The one with the largest number of infected bots was China, with more than four hundred thousand—it had the greatest number of pirated Windows Operating Systems. This was more than twice the number in Argentina, second on the list. From there, in descending order, the top twenty were India, Taiwan, Brazil, Chile, the United Kingdom, Russia, the United States, Colombia, Malaysia, Mexico, Spain, Italy, the networks of the European Union, Indonesia, Venezuela, Germany, Japan, and Korea (with just 12,292).

There were a number of theories about it. Most of those studying the worm regarded it as the work of a "dark Symantec," that is, one of the black hat "companies" in Eastern Europe funded by organized crime, probably in the Ukraine, given the Kiev connection. There was also the possibility that Conficker was a weapon, the work of a nation-state.

China was the lead suspect.

"By some estimates, there are 250 hacker groups in China that are tolerated and may even be encouraged by the government to enter and disrupt computer networks," said the 2008 U.S.–China Security Review. "The Chinese government closely monitors Internet activities and is likely aware of the hackers' activities. While the exact number may never be known, these estimates suggest that the

Chinese government devotes a tremendous amount of human resources to cyber activity for government purposes. Many individuals are being trained in cyber operations at Chinese military academies, which does fit with the Chinese military's overall strategy."

There were recent examples of China's success. Just three years earlier, Chinese hackers had stolen data from the U.S. Army Aviation and Missile Command at Redstone Arsenal, Alabama, and from NASA's Mars Reconnaissance Orbiter. "Including files on the propulsion system, solar panels, and fuel tanks," the report said. Also known to have been targeted was the Non-secure Internet Protocol Router Network (NIPRNet), an unclassified military net that handles calendars for generals and admirals, troop and cargo movements, aircraft locations and movements, aerial refueling missions, and other logistical information that a skilled analyst could use to track American military intentions and tactics. Disabling the system prior to actual combat would pose severe hardships on the American military in any conceivable war scenario.

Those who held this view saw the nod to Ukrainian keyboards and the effort to download fake AV software from *TrafficConverter.biz* as feints. The fact that Conficker had otherwise done nothing lent credence to the weapon theory. Criminals were always eager to capitalize on their breakthroughs. A nation, on the other hand, might be content to build and simply sustain a huge, stable botnet as a platform for a future digital attack.

There was still another, more hopeful, theory. What if Conficker was nothing more than a research project? Again, the fact that it had done nothing so far, along with an appreciation for malware's history, lent some weight to this view. Early infections like the Morris Worm and others were the work of graduate students showing off or testing their prowess. If some students at MIT fooling around in the lab had unleashed Conficker, they wouldn't be eager at this point to identify themselves. If this view was correct, then there was nothing to fear from the worm. What if it had been released as a demonstration of the Internet's extreme vulnerability, as a wake-up call?

There were as many theories as there were experts, because Conficker afforded few clues. Efforts to track and study the phenomenon were so uncoordinated that researchers started bumping into each other. Rick and Phil were surprised when they discovered that Chris Lee had begun sinkholing and experimenting with Conficker earlier that month at Georgia Tech. They began coordinating their efforts.

Meanwhile, Phil and Rick went sleuthing. Phil's work so far involved turning the worm's clock forward, in order to generate the domain names it would spit out in the future. He had software, called "whois," which provided identfying details of whoever had registered a domain. Phil decided to turn the clock back, to see what sites its algorithm would have generated in the weeks and months prior to its release. He figured that anyone who was going to launch something like it would probably have taken it out for a test drive first. If the launcher had done a dry run on the domain name feature, and tested linking it with a command center, that would most likely have happened recently. The exploit of Port 445 (the Chinese kit) had surfaced only the previous summer, so it was unlikely anyone would have been testing out Conficker before then. Phil ran the hybrid in his lab backward six or seven months to produce every domain name the worm would have generated in that time. Since the site names were just random arrangements of letters and numbers—it wasn't spitting out well-known domains like *espn.com* or *nytimes.com*—almost anyone who had bought one of them was likely to be their suspect, the worm's author.

He wrote to Rick:

We want to go back in time to see if there were any Conficker domains prior to release that may have been reserved for testing. Perhaps we might be able to ID the author by checking out whether they did some early testing using Internet domains that they registered directly. In short, we need some help with the "whois" lookups [identifying the identity behind the IP addresses of those testing the domains]. One thing to know is that we think the hackers are domain-tasting (i.e., they reserve the domains, which is free for 5 days, but never pay). They only need to use a given domain for a day, so they can cycle through many domains for free. Anyway, we have lots of domains, and are wondering if you can help with your "whois" capabilities.

Within a week, Rick's efforts pointed them to a distinct source. Most of the hits, 391 domain names corresponding with Conficker's random lists, were "clearly coincidental," Phil wrote an excited memo to his staff: However, I did find 9 HIGH CONFIDENCE hits. They start from Nov 27th to Dec 19th 2008.

All nine came from the same place, a website that he traced to a computer company.

"These guys are clearly the ones operating Conficker," Phil wrote.

Except, they weren't. When Phil went looking he found instead an Atlanta computer security company, Damballa, doing exactly the same thing he and Rick had been doing, running the clock backward. It was the work of Dave Dagon, who would soon join the List.

The X-Men were tripping over each other.

7

A NOTE FROM THE TRENCHES

ALL THE TRAINING . . . ALL THE PLANNING . . .
NOW IT IS TO BE PUT TO THE TEST.

—The X-Men Chronicles

T. J. Campana's birthday came three days before the end of 2008. He and his wife make a big deal out of birthdays, so he was at his home out in the Seattle suburbs. It was a family day in the middle of a holiday week, and every time T.J.'s wife caught him checking his phone for messages he would get this look.

But the messages were persistent, and they weren't all wishing him a happy birthday. For the previous month a ragtag bunch of geeks led by Phil Porras and Rick Wesson and Andre Dimino and a few others—they had begun calling themselves the Conficker Cabal—had been urging Microsoft to combat the new worm.

T.J. had listened sympathetically, but at that point this botnet was just one of many threats the software giant was watching. It was particularly interesting for a variety of technical reasons, but it had not yet eclipsed all other considerations.

The company had already patched the vulnerability the worm exploited to invade a computer, and so far customer impact had not been great enough to elevate its priority. There had been hardly any publicity about the outbreak, so there were no pressing public relations issues that might boost concern up the corporate ladder. There was the money issue, which would have to be addressed. Rick was racking up charges on his personal credit cards to buy up and sinkhole 250 domain names per day, using Amazon's S3 storage services. But there was time. As the year counted down, it was looking as if the Cabal might be able to fully contain the worm on its own.

The messages kept coming. Urgent messages. Something had happened. Still, T.J. was good. He waited until that evening, after the candles had been blown out on his cake, after the dishes had been rinsed and loaded in the washer, before begging for a few minutes of indulgence to take a closer look. What he found nearly ruined his birthday.

There was a new version of the worm, which would be dubbed Conficker B. It had started crowding into honeynets within the last twenty-four hours, and it was better than the first . . . *a lot* better. If the Tribe had been intrigued by the original version, it was now experiencing something more like respect.

For one thing, this new B strain exploded the benevolent-accident theory. Conficker was clearly not some harmless grad school lab experiment gone awry. The worm's creator had been watching every move the Cabal made, and was adjusting accordingly. If the botnet was to be strangled by cracking its domain-name-generating algorithm, learning its potential points of contact with its controller and shutting them down in advance, then why not make the effort harder? Instead of generating 250 domain names daily, and confining them to just five Top Level Domains (TLDs), Conficker B added three more TLDs: *.ws; .cn; .cc*. The designation *.cn* identified websites registered in China.

While the new variant was clearly a rewrite of the original, there were upgrades. The B strain did away with the check for a Ukrainian keyboard. It had two improved methods of spreading: (1) it searched out machines on the same network that were vulnerable before attempting to invade, and (2) it spread by the use of plug-in USB drives. It also had more security measures. Besides shutting down whatever security system was installed on the computer it invaded, and preventing communication with computer-security websites, it stopped an infected computer from downloading Windows security updates. So even in the unlikely event that the software company somehow wrangled approval to unleash some kind of anti-worm, or any sort of remediation, the infected machines would be out of reach. In addition, it modified the computer's bandwidth settings to increase speed and, thus, propagate faster still.

The first strain of Conficker had utilized Secure Hash Algorithm (SHA)-2, Ron Rivest's public encryption method, which used a public key of 1,024 bits to encode communications. This was the current Federal Information Processing Standard, which was the highest standard for public encryption. This new strain had a different encryption algorithm, and at first Hassen could not figure out what it was. It called for a 4,096-bit key, upping the level of encryption to an unprecedented level of difficulty. Hassen searched Google for Secure Hash Algorithms to match that size, and immediately found one on Rivest's website, but it was only a proposal, not a finished product. It had been proffered by Rivest in the ongoing competition to upgrade SHA-2, sponsored by the National Institute for Standards and Technology. The agency had been accepting submissions for the new standard for months. Rivest had won every previous competition, so those in the know would certainly regard his newest effort as the front-runner for SHA-3. It was not until weeks later, still stymied, that Hassen searched further, and discovered that the new strain of worm was stealing a march on the world of cryptography by employing Rivest's *proposal*. That was a shocker. How many people were even aware of these things?

This startling detail afforded another potential lead to the identity of Conficker's creator. The only way to obtain Rivest's revised proposal was to download it from his website at MIT. If the Cabal went back over Internet traffic to that website and compiled a list of those who had accessed the revised algorithm, the botmaster would have to be there. It would not be a long list, and the contents could be cross-checked with the logs of those who had visited SRI's Conficker reports, because Phil and Hassen knew that the worm's creators had been checking them. Bingo! But when they contacted Rivest, he told them that his department routinely purged the logs. It did not have a record that went back far enough.

Particularly troubling was the USB drive capability. It meant that even "closed" computer networks, those with no connection to the Internet, were vulnerable to the new strain, since users who cannot readily transmit files from point to point via the web often store and transport them on small USB drives. There had been just such a security breach at the Pentagon, one of the biggest closed networks, a notorious episode that confirmed the adage about a chain being only as strong as its weakest link. Someone had hurled fistfuls of USB drives out of a car window into a parking lot outside the gigantic military headquarters in Arlington. A defense department employee (the weak link) had picked one up off the pavement and, curious enough to be heedless, plugged it into a computer at the complex, thereby injecting a nasty virus into the large, supposedly sealed and secure military network. This had prompted a ban on all USB drives at all secure government computers (about which more later).

The USB feature was a game-changer, as far as T.J. was concerned. In the first weeks of January, Conficker B would revitalize the botnet dramatically. It began infecting more than 1.5 million new computers every day, according to an F-Secure study in mid-January. The study estimated that as of January 16, the botnet numbered 8.9 million.

The level of sophistication on the B strain wasn't just dazzling; it was scary. Out in Menlo Park, Phil and Hassen thought at first that someone else had stepped in. The worm had upped its game so expertly that it was as though the first-string team had taken over.

But there were also signs that this was the work of the same adversary. There were distinct structural similarities with Conficker A. There was also a new feature that Hassen read as a direct challenge. The B strain blocked any infected computer from accessing SRI's websites. It was as if the worm's creator had sent him a message: *We know you are after us. We'll do this to let you know that we know.* In the beginning, for Hassen, it had seemed that the botmaster lived in some parallel universe. He had no idea who he was or where he was . . . he was just *out there* somewhere, like a malevolent spirit. But with the B strain he was coming into better focus.

First of all, the botmaster was almost certainly more than one person. The worm's authors had become people, personal adversaries. They were very clever, and they were competitive, as competitive as he was. As his appreciation for their talent grew, the personal nature of their challenge really grabbed him. He found himself thinking day and night about it. The B strain showed that, so far, the botmasters had anticipated all of the Cabal's moves. They were showing off a little. Hassen knew for sure now that he was not dealing with "script kiddies," his way of thinking about pimply hackers. These guys were pros.

In Phoenix, Rodney Joffe, the Cabal's elder, also felt certain now that the worm could have been created only by a team of experts. There were simply too many levels of expertise involved; no single villain could be that proficient in so many obscure disciplines. It demonstrated deep knowledge of Windows, as if the programmer had helped write Microsoft's code, and much of the programming and packaging (as Hassen had discovered at the start) showed a fine and original hand. It showed an insider's understanding of the computer security industry worldwide, as well as a high-level understanding of Internet traffic—Rodney's own specialty. He was particularly impressed by upping from five to eight the number of TLDs tapped by its domain-name algorithm. Only people who knew exactly what they were doing would recognize how much harder that would make things for Rick Wesson and other web gurus in the group. The cryptography stuff was mind-blowing. How many people in the world were clued in to the international competition for SHA-3? It was like being a back surgeon with a rare specialty dealing with one particular vertebra, who was also a high-level astrophysicist, an astronaut, and the starting third baseman for the Philadelphia Phillies!

And it was very clear that the botmasters were watching the Cabal. Conficker B could be understood only as a countermove, and a good one.

Phil agreed. After conferring with some federal agents in Washington about the nature of the threat, he wrote a note to Rick expressing a new level of concern:

Conficker may indeed represent a multimillion-dollar business infrastructure. If they are indeed producing the kinds of revenue that we think they are, then there is a good chance they may have connections to [a] Russian or Ukranian mob. You never know, this could even have nation-state ties. If so, you realize that these folks are capable of extreme violence to those that threaten to disrupt their business. Some of the things that you've been thinking about do represent severe disruption. With that in mind, I would recommend significant discretion and anonymity. I know you're not naive about this stuff, but some of the conversations I had this week were quite eye opening for me.

T.J. began that night to address the worsened domain name problem. Rick estimated that it would now take about $100,000 per month to register all of the domain names generated by variants A and B in advance. T.J. called Ramses Martinez, the director of information security for VeriSign, Inc., a firm in Dulles, Virginia, that operated two of the thirteen root servers. It is also the registrar for some of the largest TLDs: *.com*, *.net*, and some of the country codes. He had worked with Ramses on the unsuccessful effort to contain Srizbi, which was seen as the big fish that got away. (Rick felt Ramses had, in fact, blown it on that one.) T.J. still believed the strategy against Srizbi had been correct, getting out ahead of the worm's Internet connections, but everyone involved realized that a higher level of diligence would be required if it was going to be made to work against Conficker.

"Hey, guy," he told Ramses. "*Dot-com, dot-net,* a lot of Conficker domains there."

"I knew you were going to be calling," said Ramses. Together they spoke to Pat Kane, the head of VeriSign's naming division, and agreed that they had to join the effort.

"Listen, this is the right thing to do for the Internet," said T.J.. "Let's figure out a way that we can either register or block these domains."

Given the open-ended nature of the threat, this was likely to rack up some major fees. But the three agreed to sort that problem out later. In the meantime, they set to work nailing down the next few weeks' worth of domain names that Conficker B was going to generate. T.J. was steered by Andre DiMina to Dre Ludwig, who in turn recommended that he contact Neustar, Rodney Joffe's Washington base, a clearinghouse and directory service for mobile telephone and Internet services that manages the directories for the top-level Internet domains *.us* and *.biz*, and acts as the worldwide "registry gateway" for China's *.cn* and DNS for the United Kingdom (*.uk*), Australia (*.au*),

Japan (*.jp*), and other countries.

Rodney had already been approached by Rick about getting ICANN to waive the cost of registering the worm's daily list of domains. He assured T.J., "We'll do the right thing."

Just as the Cabal felt it was getting a handle on the worm, news about the expanding botnet finally broke out of the exclusive chat rooms and websites of the computer security industry. Joel Hruska, the *Ars Technica* reporter who had somewhat complacently noted the appearance of the worm in early December, returned with a post on January 16 that noted its accelerating spread, offering the figure of 5.5 million infected computers as a "conservative estimate." John Markoff picked up the story a week later in the *New York Times,* calling Conficker "a new digital plague."

"[It] seems to be the first step of a multistage attack," he wrote. "Experts say it is the worst infection since the Slammer worm exploded through the Internet in January 2003, and it may have infected as many as nine million personal computers around the world."

Markoff quoted Rick: "If you're looking for a digital Pearl Harbor, we now have the Japanese ships steering toward us on the horizon."

Rick was not exaggerating to pump up the reporter's story. He was increasingly alarmed by Conficker's potential. On a flight back to San Francisco from Dallas on January 31, he wrote a detailed email to friends in the military and intelligence community, including John Rendon, a well-known Washington political operative who ran an information consulting firm with connections to the CIA, and who had played a critical role in lobbying for the overthrow of Iraqi dictator Saddam Hussein. The email was also sent to a top official in the DOD's Defense Intelligence Office with whom Rick had worked in the past. Rick was not alone in worrying about the seeming lack of government awareness or interest. He entitled his email "A note from the trenches," added that he hoped "this is not new news," and teased the recipients by promising, "a twisting plot of cyber warfare" and "international intrigue."

There is a botnet that has blossomed into one of the most significant threats we have faced. The methods employed are most devious. Whether developed by children or professionals they are propagating with amazing effectiveness. . . . I need your help in this defining moment in cyber security policy. . . . Today the botnet size is bounded at a low of 8 million hosts and a high of 25 million. Using the low census (note this is not an estimate, it is a measurement) of 8 million hosts: If each host were to generate a single 512 byte packet at the same time destined for a single end point, it would be a 32Gbps DDoS [a 32 gigabytes per second Directed Denial of Service attack]. A DDoS of this size would strain critical infrastructure and cause general chaos. No network attached to the Internet could mitigate a DDoS that this botnet could generate *at its lowest estimate*.

He sketched various disaster scenarios. The botnet could "take out Google or all the e-commerce on the network." A coordinated attack on Internet media outlets and websites for CNN and Fox News would shut them down for half an hour and attract worldwide attention. "Add a kinetic event [a real-world terror attack], and chaos," he said, and left to their imaginations what kind of panic such a sequence of events might arouse. He warned that the Conficker botnet could "cripple" international telephone communications, and that it was still growing. "[It] is attempting to download its second stage. . . . The second stage could do anything. . . . 8 to 25 million drones is an army even our nation-state should be worried about."

He described his scramble over the previous two months to register domains ahead of the worm daily in order to keep it from communicating with its controller.

The criminals need to register one domain out of 100,000 in the next year. They need to keep it alive for three hours to win. This is the battle. We have to be 100%; they need one out of 100,000 in the next 360 days for three hours—they win. They win a weapons-grade botnet that has penetrated many of the Fortune 500 in the USA. . . . The military is mostly clean. I'm not worried about them—everyone else is owned or getting owned. We found thousands inside companies like HP [Hewlett-Packard], Cisco, CBS. The botnet has penetrated all industries—Financial, Media, Health Care, and all levels of Federal, State, and Local government. . . . It is growing more

successfully than anything we have seen since Code Red. [It]
is the most hardened [protected] we have ever seen. . . . To
take out this botnet we need China's cooperation. Do I have
your attention?

Rick requested help in reaching out to China, and also
requested help from military computers powerful enough
to crack the worm's high-level encryption. He envisioned
this as a potential trump card. It was theoretically possible
to decipher Conficker's private key from the public key,
which Phil had extracted from both strains of the worm.
The NSA and DOD were most likely the only entities in the
world with computers powerful enough to accomplish it. If
they agreed to crack Conficker's code, the Cabal could send
orders to the botnet from any of the domains it contacted.
They would own it.

We are working to have all the domains registered by early
next week, but Microsoft is worried that something will
happen during the Super Bowl. Lots of attacks happen on
holidays; more home users leave their computers on holiday
weekends. . . . I will keep you informed as this situation
develops. I beg your assistance with a diplomatic effort with
the Chinese. I look with gleeful excitement for two private
keys that will allow us to defuse a most serious situation.

Rick was stoked about this email, and felt confident
enough that it would spur the feds into action that he

emailed T.J. privately:

> There are going to be real resources brought to bear on this bot and they are going to be looking for someone inside of MSFT [Microsoft] to decide what to do if the private keys were available. . . . How does this affect your game? policy implications?

T.J. appreciated Rick's aggressive efforts, but did not share his confidence that the feds would turn their most powerful, top-secret supercomputers to such a task. He was impressed with the level of cooperation and knowledge he saw at lower levels of law enforcement, particularly in his work with the Seattle FBI office, but he sensed that those at the highest levels of government did not fully grasp the nature of the threat.

The Defense Intelligence official who received Rick's email knew him well enough to respect his judgment. He had helped the Pentagon deconstruct Russia's cyberattacks on Estonia in 2007, and on Georgia in 2008. But how seriously should this warning be taken? Rick was seen as something of a character, brilliant but unpredictable. For a more sober assessment, Rick's email "from the trenches" was forewarded to Bill Woodcock, an internationally known Internet guru and founder of the Packet Clearing House, a web research institute based in San Francisco. Woodcock wrote back, "Yes. Conficker is serious," and then turned down the volume of Rick's alarm . . . but only a little.

> Rick's a very bright guy, smarter than me, but also
> perhaps a little more prone to getting in fights in bars than
> I am.

Woodcock estimated that the size of the potential DDoS attack projected by Rick was, in fact, probably too small, since by the time the botmaster was able to issue encrypted commands—he had not done so yet—the botnet would probably be much larger. The impact of such an attack on commercial websites would probably be less than Rick predicted, Woodcock said, but the wider impact would be far greater. Whereas Rick had specifically cited the potential for shutting down Google and the websites for news organizations, Woodcock thought that wasn't likely to happen, but not for the reason you might expect. The botnet was capable of generating such an enormous DDoS attack that the routing machinery of the Internet itself would probably crash before the specific websites could feel the brunt (harking back to the problem *TrafficConverter. biz* would have had handling the botnet's initial blitz).

> You'd get cascading failures in the core . . . impeding further
> attacks, if the full attention of a botnet of this size were
> really focused on any one target inside the U.S. That's small
> consolation for our buddies in Europe and Asia, though.

As for cracking the encryption, it was possible to decipher the private key to Conficker's code, Woodcock wrote, but inadvisable. He listed four scenarios, from best case to worst case. The best case scenario would be for "no one" to have the private key; that way the botnet could not be issued any commands. Next best would be for a single "white hat" to own the key, so that the good guys would step in and take control. Next best would be for a single "black hat" to own the key (which was apparently the present case); this was clearly not desirable but had a silver lining—because if the botmaster used it, sent instructions to the botnet, he might tip off law enforcement as to who and where he was. The worst case scenario?

> If multiple people have keys. So, although clearly things could be a lot better, they could also be a heck of a lot worse. Right now, we just have to prevent the intersection of the one party with the key, with any one of the many C&C [command and control] domains. We have to keep one unknown guy away from the many places where he could enter the launch code. In this analogy, that's a relatively simple matter of placing security around the places where the launch code could be entered.

But if the code was cracked and private keys were obtained, and then the private keys were handed over to the Cabal, then "multiple parties" would have the key, a situation "which is simply inherently much more difficult to control," Woodcock wrote. As bad as Conficker was, he argued, the present situation was more desirable. For the same reason that nuclear states strove to limit the number of countries with such arsenals, the Defense Department should worry more about the prospect of profilerating knowledge of the botnet's private keys. It was better to simply accept that one miscreant had the keys than to risk handing them over inadvertently to many.

So the U.S. government was not going to ride to the rescue. Rick received polite responses. His plea "from the trenches" was being circulated to all the appropriate agencies, the Office of the Secretary of Defense, the National Cyber Response Coordination Group (NCRCG), the U.S. Computer Emergency Readiness Team (U.S.-CERT), and a flurry of other cybersecurity-related agencies. But the upshot of it was: *Good to hear from you, thanks for calling it to the government's attention, we're fighting two wars right now . . .*

In other words, *Don't call us . . .*

Out in Menlo Park, Phil Porras decided to do more of the sleuthing he had done with Conficker A, looking to see if the author of the B variant had taken it out for a test drive before releasing it. The two strains had distinct signatures, so it was easy to tell one from the other. The very first Conficker B domain lookup would have happened on January 1, 2009. That's how the worm was programmed. Anything earlier would have to be a test run, and would have been sent by the botmaster.

When he had tried this trick with Conficker A, he had found nothing except the tinkering of another white hat researcher doing the same thing he was. But this time he found a legitimate lead. Two Conficker B–infected bots had tried to contact one of the A strain's domains on December 26, six days before the new variant showed up. The domains were *kyivstar.net,* in Kiev, and *alternativagratis.com,* which was in Buenos Aires. Kiev was the home of Baka software, and Buenos Aires was the location of Patient Zero.

No researcher even knew of the B strain until days later, so this was not another case of the X-Men stumbling into each other. This had been the botmaster playing with the new strain, checking out its communication function. It was the best lead yet on those behind the worm.

The Cabal turned over the information to the FBI, which thanked them politely . . . and then nothing happened.

8

ANOTHER HUGE WIN

REMEMBER—ABOVE ALL ELSE YOU MUST
REMEMBER TEAMWORK! YOU MUST FUNCTION AS
A ONE . . . ALWAYS!

—The X-Men Chronicles

So far the effort to curb Conficker had been pieced together on the run. The Cabal targeted a conference of Internet and security experts in early February to better organize themselves. The conference was scheduled to take place at Georgia Tech in Atlanta. The Cabal would do whatever they had to in the interim, and cook up a more formal plan of attack there.

In fact, through the month of January, the effort to contain Conficker A and B progressed well. Despite the blow of the B strain at the turn of the year, they had enough success with the strategy of getting out ahead of it, registering all of the potential command domains in advance and sinkholing all the requests from infected bots, that they started to get cocky, and began thinking ahead. With Conficker all but licked, how could they use the experience to develop a broad, coordinated strategy for the long term, something that might serve as a model for defending against future worms?

For most in the Cabal, one of the great successes so far had been the selfless approach taken by the big AV companies, all of which had set aside the profit motive to cobble together a coordinated defense. Conficker was a threat to the Internet itself, and everyone had, so far, risen to the challenge. If the AV companies began competing to market their own remedial software for the worm, the coalition was likely to crumble. So when a security company called OpenDNS unveiled a new product in early February to help clean up Conficker-infected networks, the Cabal was horrified. T.J. was particularly disappointed.

"This seriously undermines our efforts to protect users of the Internet," he wrote. The problem was not confined to "just users of the OpenDNS service," he said. He wasn't alone. Dre Ludwig, the youngest member of the Cabal, wrote:

What I would like to make sure we stay away from is "promoting" any one or multiple commercial products/services as a "golden bullet." Let's face it, there is no one solution in fact what we have is a multiple front offensive on a very dynamic chunk of malicious code.

The answer was not going to be some commercial software package aimed at protecting and purging infected networks, which had pretty much defined prior anti-malware efforts. The threat was bigger than that. It could not be attacked piecemeal, and the only hope for a broad, coordinated effort was for everyone to suspend pursuit of the almighty dollar.

The answer was going to be . . . the Cabal. Dre was one of the more expansive personalities in the Cabal, a towering man with short brown hair parted carefully on one side, a security consultant in the intel agency-heavy districts around Alexandria. Dre felt it was time to clearly define their approach:

What we need to do is make sure we get the right people involved and arming them with the right information (be it data, coordination info, etc.) and executing a plan. The plan has yet to be formulated to any extent beyond "let's do something" as far as I have seen. We have plenty of the right people on this list and plenty more parties that are joining this merry band every day. Let us not rush into things by promoting solutions, ideas, thoughts, etc. as the answer. Let us try and effectively share and collaborate on ideas and build out a proper plan of attack.

I think the first thing that we should do is continue to focus on snatching up domains for this thing. This effectively buys us time and wrangles some form of control on the spread of this thing. Our second order should be to sort out exactly who is a part of this group, and follow up with who else needs to be involved. Once we have a handle on that we should then proceed to sort out a plan of attack to utilize all the resources we have mustered (commercial/press/LE [law enforcement]/etc.). . . . Each individual will have a different perspective on things, as we produce and share these perspectives we can more effectively hash out a solution that encompasses all of our experiences and viewpoints. So again, let's focus on forward momentum without getting stuck in the trap of brash movements or decisions that could compromise our young coalition.

T.J. agreed.

We need to start taking the Internet back from these bad guys . . . Well, now it is a full-blown reaction force and we are doing great things . . . learning a lot . . . but there is a long way to go. I keep saying this, "We have to be right 500 times a day . . . they just need to be right once." Oh yeah . . . we want to find these guys and put them in jail . . . more on that later :-)

The Atlanta conference would be the first time some of the Cabal met—in person, that is. In some ways their online personas were more real than the flesh-and-blood versions, since they tended to live in front of their monitors. The Conficker mission was something distinct from the conference itself, of course, which was a mouthful: the First Annual Global DNS Security, Stability, and Resiliency Symposium. It had been set up by ICANN as a way of discussing any and all issues related to the ever-growing malware problem. The nonprofit international agency had only a narrowly defined role to play, assigning and keeping track of "Names and Numbers" on the Internet, and had no power to make or enforce policy, but it was the closest thing there was in the world to an international governing body. The worm was a new and major concern, and was clearly the front line of the larger battle, but it was not on the official agenda. It had not been around long enough for there to be completed studies and reports, but it was the primary buzz in the symposium corridors. Rodney Joffe had already been in touch with ICANN about eliminating the costs associated with registering domains, and invited the organization's reps to a rump meeting during the conference. It would be Rodney's first official act for the Cabal. They met after hours in a conference room at a nearby Holiday Inn where some of the conventioneers were staying off the Georgia Tech campus.

They convened in a long, narrow hotel conference room with tables arranged in a horseshoe. The Holiday Inn had to move them to a larger room at the last minute. It seemed everybody wanted in. There was even an FBI agent in attendance, a real coup for the Cabal. The tables were covered with starched white linen, with bowls of hard candy set at intervals. A speakerphone was placed in the center of the room inside the U-shaped table arrangement, so that those who weren't in Atlanta could participate. The session lasted for almost two hours. Rodney was there, of course, as were Dre Ludwig and Chris Lee, who brought beer. Andre Di Mino and various others participated by phone hookups. The guests of honor in the room were Paul Twomey, the head of ICANN; John Crain, one of his colleagues; and the FBI man, of course. It was clear that long-term global efforts to contain the worm would require more formal involvement from both agencies.

It was late afternoon across the continent on Microsoft's campus in Redmond, where T.J. participated via telephone from his office high in one of the sprockets. He just listened for a while, and then, when he was introduced, explained how the registry-buying strategy worked.

"I think the overriding issue at this point is, you know, there's a question about the fee that they have to pay to ICANN in order to get these," he said. "That could quickly become unsustainable if they're being asked to register, you know, we're asking at this point to register two hundred and fifty domains per day, in perpetuity. This is obviously for the common good."

Twomey didn't need much convincing. His feeling was that the threat required an "alliance of response." But something in his words conveyed an opposite impression to T.J., who thought the president of ICANN was waffling, and called him on it loudly.

"This is the future of the Internet," he declaimed over the speakerphone, his vehemence gaining everyone's attention. "This is the line in the sand, guys. If we're not gonna draw the line and we're gonna let this pass, we're setting the stage for kind of the next ten years of people abusing DNS—"

"Whoaa, whoa, whoa!" interrupted Twomey. "We're on board!"

T.J. apologized.

The issues were: How do you register domains en masse? How do you arrange to just taste those domains, instead of purchasing them outright? Twomey dialed his legal staff in Marina Del Ray right from the meeting room, and instructed them to find a way in the rules for ICANN to allow the Cabal to make rapid, unilateral decisions. There would be no charge to register the Conficker domain names. Twomey recognized that Conficker was a turning point. It was a threat that demanded that the worldwide community of Internet providers function for the first time not as a loose confederation of interests, but as a single community.

He delegated the job of working with the Cabal to his subordinate, Crain, who quickly accepted. Back in his Redmond office, listening, T.J. thought, . . . *Sure, boss, I'll save the Internet. Just let me get my cape here out of the locker!*

The biggest immediate problem was tying up domain names in China, *.cn,* one of the new Top Level Domains. China was problematic for a number of reasons. For those who suspected Conficker was the work of a nation-state, or perhaps of contractors at work for a nation-state, China

167

topped the list of suspects.

As we have seen, intelligence experts believed China was regularly hacking into sensitive U.S. government networks, including some used by the Pentagon. The network controlling the electric grid for the United States had also experienced incursions. Just looking at the sophistication of Conficker, some people found it hard to believe that anyone other than a nation—and by "a nation," they meant China every time—to have created the worm.

So China was a sensitive subject. And now the Cabal was in the position of having to ask China's help to contain the monster. Most in the Holiday Inn meeting room were stymied. Whom do you call? Whom do you ask? Do you want to ask? How could they collaborate with a government that rejects the very notion of a techno utopia? Rejects the ideal of *free information*, the founding principle of the Internet? China operated outside the fence, so to speak. It was the largest and most powerful of the wired countries that unapologetically monitored and censored. How do you even talk to these people? How do you ask them for help? But with the majority of Conficker bots in China, how could you pull this thing off without them?

"I know a guy there," offered Crain, a Brit who had a home in Long Beach but basically lived out of a suitcase. "Let's see if we can get an email to him. Figure out on the phone what we'll do."

They tried calling the Chinese offical right away, but

there was no answer. It turned out to be the Chinese New Year. Twomey eventually spoke personally to the head of China's Network Information Center, which governed the Internet there, and secured his full cooperation. Everyone at the Georgia Tech conference left feeling surprised and impressed by Twomey's swift response. The Cabal felt they were really getting somewhere. With typical enthusiasm and floridity, soon after the meeting, Dre Ludwig posted to the List:

> I cannot stress how important and amazing it is what this group has accomplished (and is still accomplishing). As far as I know this is the first time there has been this level of involvement from so many different groups (from ICANN, to Microsoft, to the FBI, to all the affected registries, to the AV community, even to ISPs! Now what we need to do is cement the message we want the world to hear, and effectively communicate that. This in my eyes is ANOTHER HUGE win for the good guys. . . . I cannot speak for T.J. or his organization, but based on the talks we have had prior to this mess I don't think there will be any issues moving forward. . . . Everything we are doing and have done is a sum of everyone's efforts, and the message as I have heard it has always been one of cooperation between the various industries and groups. . . . What we are doing here as a group in my view at least is a CRITICAL process being to build and flush out for the entire health of the Internet. We need to make sure that moving forward this process of sharing information, and capabilities between the various industries we have assembled here grows. WE RUN AND OWN THE

INFRASTRUCTURE, and we all need to understand that the only way to defend it against abuse is to cooperate with the various industries that have different insights into the larger problem. . . . I just want to honestly tell everyone who has been a part in this that I personally thank them for their effort, their resources, their patience, and their cooperation. If it wasn't for every single individual who has been involved in this to this point we would be stuck with distribution of efforts that would at best be short lived, and at worst disruptive to everyone. I think I owe everyone a beer or three the next time I see them.

Soon after the Atlanta meeting, Microsoft offered a $250,000 reward for identifying the person or persons behind Conficker. This is when the group also formally dubbed itself the Conficker Working Group (CWG). It sounded more respectable than the Cabal. Some felt that the word "cabal," with its sinister connotation, conveyed the wrong impression. In all of its future official communications, the group became CWG. Of course, disavowing a nickname is the surest way to make it stick. Everyone, including those on the List, continued calling it the Cabal.

There was such a clamor to get involved, especially when the press got hold of the story, that subgroups were created for various and sundry aspects of the botnet: these subgroups included a large one to analyze the malware itself, another to study and maintain the sinkholing, another to handle the DNS problem, and so on. The Cabal's List was reserved for the cream. They were, after all, the X-Men.

Whatever the title, the approach seemed to be working. To Dre, in another email from this week, their mission was "too important to fail." The FBI agent who had been at the Holiday Inn session remarked, "We need to find a way to do this kind of thing in other cases, this issue around domains, because this is probably not going to be the last time it happens."

The agent had not come to Atlanta out of national concern for Conficker. Rodney had just cornered him that morning and urged him to attend, as part of the continuing efforts of the Cabal to get the feds to pay attention.

Working together was something new for most of those involved. Most of the X-Men had achieved their current level of expertise on their own, and they came at cybersecurity with interests that occasionally conflicted. Pure researchers like Phil Porras, consultants like Dre Ludwig, and botnet vigilantes like Andre DiMino eyed their entrepreneurial colleagues and those employed by the big security companies with more than a little suspicion. The data being collected about the botnet had serious and growing commercial value. Participation in the Cabal might better position an AV company to cash in down the road. There was also considerable prestige attached now to the effort in the cybersecurity world. The press was growing increasingly interested in the worm, and some members of the Cabal, particularly those who had long-standing relationships with reporters like the *New York Times'* John Markoff or Brian Krebs, felt daily pressure to spill details of the group's efforts, and tended to get their names prominently mentioned. This did not sit well with others in the Cabal, who disdained self-promotion, and who recognized that leaks of any kind would help the botmasters, who were clearly paying attention to the Cabal's every move.

With few exceptions—like T.J. at Microsoft and Phil at SRI—members of the group were volunteers, ostensibly motivated by a sense of public purpose, by commitment to the idea of the Internet, and by the sheer excitement of the challenge. Most were fitting in work on Conficker around their day jobs, figuring the contacts they made and the things they learned couldn't hurt them, and buoyed by a sense of doing the right thing. But suspicions started to grow that not everyone was so idealistically motivated.

These doubts came to a head when it was discovered that Rick Wesson had, on his own, decided to reach out to China.

It was typical of him. Rick had a well-known maverick disposition, an aggressive approach to problem solving, and—the propensities were related—a talent for annoying people. He also had a puckish sense of humor, as when, early on, he had started registering all of the Conficker domains in the name of the FBI's top cybersecurity agent—a none-too-subtle hint that maybe Washington should be paying more attention. The Bureau was not amused.

When *.cn* showed up as one of the new Top Level

Domains generated by Conficker B, Rick had acted swiftly to solve the problem. In a move reminiscent of the one that had earned him an F on his undergrad project at Auburn, he went ahead and reached out directly to the Chinese, handing over access to the data he had been sinkholing for months. It made perfect sense to him. Given that so many of the Conficker bots were in China, it would not have been hard for the country's Internet snoopers to acquire much of the information themselves, at least going forward. So it never occurred to Rick that sharing what he and Chris Lee at Georgia Tech had collected would cause a problem. As he saw it, it built goodwill between China and the rest of the world, and it would help solve the Conficker problem, both the Internet's and his own.

China kept its official hands clasped tightly around the Internet's throat. Authoritarian societies are unquestionably better at some things than democratic ones, so if China decided to help, it could be counted on to do a good job of tracking and rerouting the botnet's traffic. This would take the largest single portion of the botnet out of play. So Rick reached out directly to Xiaodong Lee of China's Internet Network Information Center. He had another good reason to act quickly. He could not foresee that ICANN would waive the fees. On the last day of January alone he had charged $5,000 to his American Express card to register *.cn* domains. His estimates of how much the work and fees had cost his company threatened to top $100,000.

Microsoft had balked at reimbursing him. T.J. wrote to him that the numbers were "well outside the ballpark" of what the software giant was prepared to pay. So China's help would relieve some of the pressure there. A win-win, as far as Rick was concerned.

Unfortunately many in the Cabal did not see it the same way. Most of Rick's colleagues were appalled. There was plenty about their effort they were not eager to share with China. For one thing, they had discovered a flaw in the programming for Conficker B that made all of the bots it infected vulnerable to hijacking by a third party—either the good guys or a rival miscreant. One of the worm's tactics was to patch the vulnerability at Port 445, so that no rival exploit could attack it. The newer strain of worm had an error in this part of its code, which meant that anyone who owned a list of infected computers, if he could exploit the mistake, might be able to hijack the entire botnet. The exploiter would have to figure out a way to insert his own code, an effort that would ultimately fail, but at the time there were high hopes for it. It was one of the Cabal's most closely held secrets. If Rick was out there sharing sinkholed data on his own, what else was he sharing? What if the Chinese government figured it out first? Given that there were scores of sensitive U.S. government networks, not to mention banking and corporate networks, on the list of infections, who would want the Chinese government in possession of a tool to remotely control them? And given that China was high on the list of suspects behind the worm, why would anyone with the public interest at heart just hand over detailed information about the Cabal's effort against it?

Dre Ludwig, in particular, was furious. Had Rick *sold* the data? He was already under suspicion by some in the Cabal of trying to capitalize on his insider knowledge. Everyone knew that Rick was a friend of David Ulevitch, the founder and CEO of OpenDNS, the company that had so alarmed the Cabal by marketing its own Conficker remedy. Dre smelled a rat. It was exactly the kind of thing he expected from those in the Cabal whom he called, disparagingly, "businessmen." After all, Rick was in the business of selling data to paying customers, precisely the kind of thing that, say, Shadowserver's Andre DiMino was against philosophically; it went back to his hypothetical question: *If you knew someone's house was in danger of catching on fire, would you simply warn him or offer to sell him the information?*

Dre Ludwig was every bit as much of a purist, and was also unyielding and confrontational in a way the other Andre was not. His rise in his field had been rapid since he flunked out of high school in California. He had taken vocational computer courses at a community college, and found work putting his formidable programming skills to use for several companies near home, where, like T.J. Campana and Andre DiMino, he got his first taste of the malware wars. He was hooked. The contest tapped his competitive core: *These*

175

people think they're smarter than me? And he spent the next ten years accumulating credentials and a reputation. After working for a time with Rodney Joffe at Neustar as a tech wunderkind, Dre had set himself up as an independent consultant in the rich turf of Alexandria, where for someone with his skills government contracts were as plentiful as pink cherry blossoms in springtime. He was brash and cocky. He stood big belly forward and small head back, and had a way of fixing you with a steady brown-eyed stare before saying something outrageous.

He had no illusions about the Cabal. He saw all the different motivations, personal and professional, and he had no big problem with them in principle. But Dre drew the line at the point where these private motivations trumped the overarching goal. He was tipped off to Rick's Chinese outreach when a fellow researcher noticed some Chinese IP addresses popping up on logs and servers of the Cabal's subgroups. He emailed Dre, "Dude, do you know what your boy is doing?"

Dre thought he knew exactly what "his boy" was doing. He guessed that Rick was leveraging his insider access, the data, and his knowledge to execute a project with whomever over there, without concern for anything but his own gain. That, for him, as he told a friend, "Is like you're pissing in my pool, dude. Don't piss in my pool and tell me it's lemonade. Like, fuck you, dude." This was now alpha-geek stuff. Who did Rick think he was? It aggravated another, subtler divide in the Cabal. As its youngest member, Dre felt squarely on the youthful side of the X-Men. He and grad student Chris Lee at Georgia Tech had more in common with the teams of geeks who were now flocking into the Cabal's various subgroups than with their fellows on the List. To them, despite his youthful style, Rick was one of the elders, someone who had achieved a big reputation in their field just for showing up early. There was a fear that the volunteer labor being performed by the younger element out of an idealistic commitment was going to be exploited by the elders for their own profit. This was the nerve struck by word that Rick was dealing with China on his own. *Fuck it,* thought Dre; *this dude's crossed the line for me. I'm going to put him on blast.*

On T.J.'s next conference call, when the subject came up, Dre lost it. Not right away. He listened for a while. Everyone was being very polite and upbeat. Chris Lee was listening on his cell phone as he walked to work across the Georgia Tech campus. He knew Dre wanted him to join in blasting Rick, but he resisted, hoping Rick would explain himself satisfactorily. Dre thought: *Nobody else is saying shit,* he thought. *No one else seems to care.* Then he started peppering Rick with direct questions: Who are you talking to? What data are you giving them?

When he found the answers evasive, he exploded, making sure everyone could feel his anger—the word *prick* was used.

"What are you doing?"

"Why did you do this?"

"Did you understand the impact? What you're effectively doing is handing over, you know, potentially control of millions of people's home PCs to effectively unknown parties!"

He didn't get direct answers. Dre left the meeting more convinced than ever that Rick was not only capitalizing on all of their work for his own profit, but undercutting the effort in the process. Rick had afterward emailed Andre DiMino, the even-tempered, universally respected head of Shadowserver, and asked, "Man . . . what did I do to Dre?"

Andre, ever the soul of diplomacy, just responded by sending Rick a passage from a note Dre had posted earlier, which strongly suggested that he and his hotheaded young compatriot were on the same page:

We are all on the same team, we may have different motivations/views/angles/perspectives/religions/sexual preferences/favorite colors/favorite foods/etc. but in the end WE RUN/OWN the infrastructure and the bad guys just wish they did. So let's put our differences aside for a little while and get things done and try not to let things devolve. There should only be one motivation at play within this group and that should be focusing on mitigation of this threat, and setting a precedent for future threats (processes/contacts/relationships/ etc.). Everything else just gets in the way and does our (note the use of that word) cause no good. So let's all try and set

aside our egos, profit motives, and past experiences with each
other for a little while so we can do what has never been done
before.

Rick denied it all, vehemently, but Dre was not the only
member of the Cabal who wondered. If he had not in fact sold
the data, had he offered it in hopes of currying favor with the
despots, in hopes of doing lucrative business with them down
the road? For some the fact that he had acted alone and in a
way that struck them as furtive confirmed his guilt.

In the end, it was this last question that prompted a
move to oust Rick from the Cabal. He was pressed to
divulge everything he had given to the Chinese, and to
acknowledge that he had violated his privileged position
in the group by acting without putting the matter to a
vote. There was no way to prove he had profited from
his approach to China, but there was no getting around
the fact that he handed the Chinese the keys to valuable
data without getting permission from the others. Some of
their membership, especially the lurking feds, had security
clearances to protect. If they were members of the Cabal,
and the Cabal was sharing information with China, did that
make them complicit in leaking sensitive data? They felt that
at the very least they should have been consulted. To some
in the inner circle it smelled like betrayal.

Dre posted his complaint formally to the List, where
he tried to state his concerns in a more restrained

fashion—avoiding singling out Rick, for one:

> Was everyone aware of this change? Was every party that is a part of this process represented in the decision making process? . . . The reason why I am raising this point is that it would appear that a few members of the group made a call that affects every individual and organization that has publicly stated that they are a part of this process. There are very real implications to various organizations' reputation if this group or process falls apart. . . . No matter what any one group or individual wants to think they do not own this process, they are not the sole provider of the capabilities that are utilized in this process, nor are they the "deciders." They are only merely cogs of varying criticality in a much larger machine whose importance is greater than any one part. . . . Unfortunately we are now in a WHOLE NEW REALM of scrutiny for each of us as individuals, as participating groups, and as a larger group. . . . I am not calling into question the validity of the decision to move the data, or the location it is being moved to. What I am calling into question is the buy-in of the entire group. . . . Everything needs to be laid out in the open and there should be strict guidelines for transparency in place. . . . This also calls into question issues of ownership of the data that is produced. Do the individuals who are sucking up the data own it? What are the guidelines for distribution and use of the data, are they outlined beyond just various conference calls and gentlemen's agreements, nods, and winks? This sort of wiggle room produces the opportunity for this process to get sideways and off track in a very quick and real manner. Avoidance of such a

situation should be everyone's number one priority! I am sorry for such a long-winded and "heavy" email, but I wanted to make sure at the very minimum I expressed my own personal thoughts and worries with the group as a whole. These very issues are very familiar to me due to my involvement with other industry groups and private groups where they have appeared before. They are very important to properly think through and deal with as the scale of the task we are undertaking here is on such a scale as to be nearly impossible to grasp or quantify. This is due to the fact that we aren't solving technical problems, we are in essence addressing societal issues that have direct impact on technical controls. If you need evidences of this simply look how quickly the technical controls were put in place vs. how long it took to get the right people's ears.

On a sunny day in February, Paul Vixie met with Rick on a bench in San Francisco's Yerba Buena Gardens, atop the Moscone Convention center. It got touchy. Paul was there to act as a mediator, but Rick was insulted to be confronted again by unfounded suspicions. Paul was mostly in agreement with Rick's reasoning for sharing the data, but pointed out that, as part of the group, Rick really ought to have consulted with the others beforehand.

Tempers cooled in subsequent days. Rick was never booted from the Cabal. But the sinkhole operation was consolidated with Chris Lee at Georgia Tech. Rick continued to play an active role, but never fully emerged from the cloud of suspicion.

Despite these occasional flare-ups, by the end of February the Cabal was feeling pretty good about itself. There was a growing sense that Conficker was contained, or very nearly. There was some talk about preparing a postmortem on the whole project. They all agreed that this was a watershed battle. They wanted their triumph remembered. There was a lot of credit to be shared, and there were lots of reasons for grabbing some of it. So in addition to the reward money, members of the Cabal agreed to start pushing for press coverage. It was a good idea to let the world know how dangerous this botnet was potentially, and about how all these members of the Tribe had come together on their own in a selfless effort to combat it. Their efforts at first produced only a trickle of coverage in the mainstream press. The subject matter was just too esoteric for most . . . at first. Once they started that ball rolling downhill, it would continue to pick up speed. The heightened press attention did attract scores of botnet hunters eager to join the battle. Since its beginning, back in early December, the battle against Conficker had grown from an initial core of fewer than a dozen, to, when you counted all the new subgroups, more than three hundred. As it appeared the project was closing in on final success, involvement was a feather in any geek's cap, whether in academia, industry, or government. This was cutting-edge stuff, and the effort was . . . well, there was no other word for it: *heroic!*

By early March, millions of Conficker A and B bots were

in check. China was handling its Conficker problem with ruthless efficiency. Each of the millions of bots was checking in regularly to the scores of domains generated daily, and nearly all of these requests were now being routed directly to the sinkhole at Georgia Tech, where members of the Cabal could count, observe, and analyze them.

What they had accomplished was amazing, but it still wasn't good enough. In his cheerleading email in early February, T.J. had written: "The fact that we have so many people willing to help is a WIN! We are sink-holing a ton of traffic for analysis . . . WIN! We know a lot about this threat based on analysis done by many people on this thread . . . WIN!"

Dripping with sarcasm, Rick had promptly responded, "This is really filling *my* sails," and reminded everyone, "We had over 99% yesterday . . . only 100% counts." They were edging closer to that goal.

And still Conficker had done nothing. When the B strain appeared, most of the Cabal assumed it was about to take action in some way. This is what had prompted Rick's alarm "from the trenches" to the Defense Department. It looked as though the enormous botnet was about to wake up.

But then . . . *nothing*. It did not make sense. The mystery around the worm deepened. Who was behind Conficker? What was it for?

Toni Koivunen, a Finnish analyst with F-Secure, wrote that he found the lack of profiteering by Conficker "simply amazing."

The creators of this botnet are curiously not interested in the (likely millions) a network of this size could reap for spam delivery, credit card fraud, etc. Yet the world's spam traps are not dry, phish scams are plentiful, and there appear to be no market inefficiencies in employing other recent and revived botnets for spam delivery. If they wanted to use [Conficker] for spam, there are buyers. We may put aside for now the "fake AV" feint [the programmed original contact with *Trafficconverter. biz*]. We may also put aside the interesting notion (mentioned in some circles) that this was a spam botnet, but it exceeded the authors' expectations in terms of size, and cannot be managed. . . . This botnet, in terms of unique IPs (not just hosts), is by conservative estimates solidly in the million-host level. This is orca huge; yet supposedly it just sits there?

Conficker's dormancy fed the theory that it was really a weapon. A nation-state wanting to arm itself for almost any kind of cyberattack could do no better than a vast, stable botnet. It could be used to launch anything. But if this was so, wouldn't they have been smart enough to disguise it better? In some ways, creating something this big without using it invited a level of attention anyone in this game would prefer to avoid.

Rick wrote:

It is my current hunch that this is not a botnet run by cyber criminals. This one is curiously "idle," like no others have been before. If this one does turn out to be state-sponsored, I would give it high marks for penetration, but a low score for its present failure to act like a criminal spam botnet. And so I'm in the unexpected position of actually hoping this one sends spam. At least that suggests a class of adversary with familiar, economic goals.

Tying up the domains generated every day might keep Conficker from doing anything, but it would not stop the worm from spreading. Would the Cabal tire of the time, effort, and expense involved with registering scores of new ones every day? They had sustained it for two full months now. Were they prepared to keep doing it for additional months? For years? Maybe this, too, was part of the botmaster's strategy. If the botnet was built for the long term, the botmaster could afford to wait until the Cabal's interest and patience were exhausted.

Meanwhile, more and more major computer networks were discovering the invader. There were headlines worldwide, marking invasions large and small. In the United Kingdom, the Defense Ministry and Parliament had been hit. So had the military computer networks for France and Germany. The Houston municipal court. Southwest Airlines. The Greater Manchester Police. India and Brazil had huge outbreaks. By the end of February 2009, estimates of how far and wide the botnet spread varied, with some security companies placing the number between ten million and twelve million.

But alarm still generated only an off-key response.

Ironically, the biggest actual problem it posed so far came when organizations acted to get rid of it. It wasn't all that hard to kill, but banks, government agencies, and corporations incurred tremendous cost and inconvenience shutting down their networks for the procedure. For many, it was easier to simply leave Conficker alone than to attack it; this, too, may have been part of the worm's genius.

Techies were getting used to it. Someone posted a playful poem to the geek discussion board Slashdot on February 20.

> If you're on the highway and Conficker goes beep beep,
> Just step aside or you might end up in a heap.
> Conficker, Conficker runs on the road all day.
> Even the coyote can't make him change his ways.
> Conficker, the coyote's after you.
> Conficker, if he catches you you're through.
> Conficker, the coyote's after you.
> Conficker, if he catches you you're through.
> That coyote is really a crazy clown,
> When will he learn he can never mow him down?
> Poor little Conficker never bothers anyone,
> Just runnin' down the road's his idea of having fun.

Everybody got a kick out of the poem. But if the rest of world was merely whelmed, the X-Men knew better. All it would take was one successful connection to turn cute catastrophic. All they had to do was miss one domain, one command. In the *New York Times*, Markoff called Conficker "a ticking time bomb."

Then, on March 6, the worm turned.

9

MR. JOFFE GOES TO WASHINGTON

TODAY A MASSIVE SHADOW FALLS ACROSS THE
CITY . . . AND FEAR BECOMES A REALITY.
—The X-Men Chronicles

The news hit the List early Friday evening, March 6.

"Greetings to all," posted Dean Turner, a Symantec analyst. "As some of you may be aware, we've identified a new variant."

Phil Porras got the news in a phone call, and immediately tapped out a summary and marching orders to his team. They would all be working over the weekend:

> Guys,
> Results from the Phone:
>> —SRI, Symantec, MS are taking the reverse engineering lead.
>> —Media blackout til at least Mon, til we know what to say
>> —How does it work

—What's our plan to block it

—Do we have signatures/

—We need a thoughtful understanding of

—what are the DNS/Network mitigation strategies

—how can we collect future Conficker telemetry

—Forensic details of how this works

—Any and every detail to help fight it

The really bad news came almost simultaneously. Jose Nazario, a well-known computer security expert working for Arbor Networks, posted:

Save everyone the browsing trouble. Highlights: 50,000 domain names a shot instead of 250.

Fifty thousand domain names per day? The Cabal had scrambled and fought and cajoled to preregister 250 domain names per day. The effort had strained their relationships and Rick Wesson's credit cards. It had required unprecedented international cooperation, coordinated by ICANN, which was not set up for this kind of thing. Getting 250 domains per day locked down had been considered a triumph.

But fifty thousand? It was flat-out diabolical! Conficker C was programmed to kick in on April 1, upping the ante so high that . . . well, after you gasped you almost had to laugh. Infected machines were to check in for commands on that date. To prevent the worm from making contact with its controller, the Cabal would have to identify and register all fifty thousand, and this would mean tracking down those that were already owned worldwide, and coaxing their owners into shutting down for a few days. And they would have to do that *every day* from April 1 forward. How in the world were they supposed to do that?

"F&*king Hell," posted Rodney Joffe, from his office in Phoenix.

Dave Dagon of Georgia Tech was struck by what it would mean if they somehow pulled it off.

> Have we got the grapes to ask for the removal of 50K domains per day? That would signal to the botmaster this organization is using policy, and not money, to accomplish this goal. It may end this cat-mouse run, or escalate further. . . . This is interesting times, folks.

Rodney quickly followed up with another note, just ticking off the issues that occurred to him immediately. At least some of the the TLDs involved might simply decide to draw the line—anticipating that even if the Cabal could corral Conficker C, what would stop the botmaster from introducing D? Then E? Then F?

> I suspect that some of the TLDs will be forced to say, "We can't possibly cope with D [whatever ridiculous number the botmaster might crank Conficker up to next], so we don't want to have to ramp up just to deal with C if there's no exit strategy." We knew it would happen. Now it has. What's plan C?

Out in his office in the Redmond sprocket, T. J. Campana scheduled an immediate conference call, and attempted to rally the demoralized troops in an email:

> We either take the fight to them or go home at this point. I vote that we try . . . and when they go for 100,000 we try that. . . . We are being tested people. The DNS [Domain Name System] infrastructure is being tested. . . . Let's get this thing reversed and at the very least try.

As details of the new variant emerged—Phil and his staff, working straight through the weekend in Menlo Park, produced a remarkable portrait of its anatomy in record time—there was even more consternation.

Rodney lamented:

> The techniques employed should scare us since they are the next evolutionary step. We knew early on that our mitigation technique for A/B wasn't going to work at the next level, and now it's been demonstrated. (I don't hold out hope [of all the TLD] operators being able to hear us, much less trust us, much less add this burden to their workload, much less do so in an error free manner.)

The X-Men began to doubt themselves.

"This is starting to stink of an inside job," wrote a security geek at Bell Aliant, the Canadian telecommunications company.

"I am going to repeat here what I have said privately," wrote Rodney. "The people behind this are us."

This cryptic line set some of the more literal-minded in the Cabal to speculating that Conficker's author was, in fact, *one of them*. Rodney promptly explained that what he meant was this: the sort of people behind the worm were the same sort of people as those in the Cabal. They were gifted, experienced, and hardworking *fellow mutants*. And what's more, they had a built-in advantage in this game. They were on the offense. The botmaster had just waited for the Cabal to make a move, like, say, tying up all 250 domains generated by the worm every day, and then had boosted the worm's algorithm, and the level of difficulty, into the stratosphere.

"How do we level the playing field?" asked Rodney.

Ever the ray of sunshine, Paul Vixie shot back:

We don't. We lose. Now that we've LOST and/or we know WE WILL LOSE, we decide how to carve up the Internet into defensible neighborhoods and leave the rest to the drug lords. It'll be like *Escape from New York,* except our gated community will be on the inside, not the outside.

In the midst of this general shock and awe, Dave Dagon suggested that it was time to seek help:

If we go this route [trying to corral Conficker C], I suspect we'd need high level engagements: Dept. of State—to address the

questions, "Why should our country help your Cabal?" DOJ—
reprioritize the Conficker investigation. DHS/US-CERT—for all
the SIGINT [Signals Intelligence] out there, I do hope someone
has insight into the creators of this botnet, and can take action
before further critical infrastructure is impacted. . . . Call this
weekend and warn our friends.

It was definitely time to shake the feds into action. From the beginning of this effort the Cabal had politely shared data with the appropriate government agencies, those charged with cybersecurity and law enforcement. To all of the X-Men it seemed that the efforts had been exclusively one-way. Whatever they fed the alphabet soup just disappeared into its giant maw. Nothing ever came back out. Here the Cabal were busting their collective butts, working overtime and on weekends, racking their brains, tapping every source and contact they had worldwide, battling to save the Internet . . . where were the people who got paid to do this?

Rodney packed for Washington.

When Phil and his team were ready with their full report on Conficker C on Tuesday, the prospect had never looked worse. C-Day, the day the new strain would wake up and seek instructions, was just twenty-one days away.

The original strain of the worm had a domain generating algorithm that spread its 250 potential command and control locations over five TLDs. Conficker B had made things more difficult by adding three more TLDs to the mix, which meant Rick Wesson and John Crain of ICANN and the others had to bargain with eight. Conficker C pulled out all the stops. Not only was it going to spit out fifty thousand potential domains daily, but they would be spread out over every country TLD in the world, 110 of them, and six more besides, for a total of 116 TLDs!

It got even worse. As Hassen Saidi broke into the new strain, he noticed that there was a scrambled section in the code for this new algorithm. Whatever was hidden in this obfuscated section, it was causing an infected computer to open several ports that controlled communications. There was every kind of speculation about what this meant, but no one could decipher it.

Again, for Hassen, the challenge was personal. The botmaster had handed him another puzzle. The segment of code in question was unreadable in any of the computer languages he knew, so he began the painstaking process of breaking the source code down to object code, the basic ones and zeros of machine language. It took him three weeks. It turned out to be very simple, even elegant. The worm's creator had designed an original peer-to-peer protocol.

With the first two strains, every infected computer in the botnet had to contact the right domain in order to receive instructions. In effect, the botmaster sat behind one of the many doors and doled out instructions to each bot individually. He had to, in effect, touch every one. This was a relatively inefficient way to disseminate a command. Peer-to-peer greatly simplified the process. Bots could now talk directly to each other. The botmaster had to touch only one machine. So long as one received the command, it could spread the message on its own. Conficker machines infected with C were just pinging each other, asking, "Hey, do you have a copy? Do you have a file for me?"

It occurred immediately to the Cabal that this peer-to-peer innovation might afford them an opening. They were running Conficker bots in any number of honeypots now. Why not poison the botnet by having one of their own use the new direct method of communication to spread some worm-crippling code? It would be less invasive than trying to push corrective software to infected machines over the Internet, and not the white hats but the worm itself would be reaching into the bots. But as Hassen looked deeper, he saw that the worm's authors were one step ahead again. They had anticipated the move. They had designed their peer-to-peer protocol to be cagey. The connected computers compared lists of twenty-five Conficker bots—*These are the people I know, by the way.* This gave both computers fifty potential domains to choose from, and each chose only one. Each was programmed to favor its own list over those it obtained from the other. The upshot was that any attempt by the Cabal to drop a poisoned seed into the botnet would spread glacially, at best. Again, Hassen was impressed.

In a way, the fifty thousand domains per day, the piece

of the new strain that caused so much alarm, may have just been a diversion. Peer-to-peer was the real innovation. Hassen could now put himself inside the head of the worm's creator. Why not freak out the Cabal by giving them an impossible task? Send them chasing all over the world to tie up fifty thousand domains every day. And then quietly slip in the *real* zinger, the peer-to-peer protocol, which was far worse. After all, even the best efforts of the Cabal to preregister the 250-domain daily output of Conficker B had been beatable. The new strain had spread from one of the domains missed by Rick and John and the others helping them. Rick had warned continually that 99 percent wasn't good enough, and he had been proved right. On the worm's daily list of domain names, which was just randomly generated strings of letters, every once in a while there were domains that were real, that had already been registered. It was easy to assume that the botmaster would not be so bold as to preregister a domain that every white hat security geek in the world was watching, but that's exactly what he had done, right under the Cabal's nose. The botmaster had won that game. And if he could pull that off with a 250-per-day scheme, why did he need fifty thousand?

There was another astonishing new wrinkle. Everyone had been impressed by the unique high-level encryption method utilized by Conficker B. The worm's creators had adopted—really, they had been the first to ever adopt—the Secure Hash Algorithm proposed by MIT professor

Ron Rivest in the international contest to establish a new, higher standard for public encryption—SHA-3. This was to ensure that no one could hijack the botnet; only the worm's author had the keys to that code. In the months since Rivest had originally crafted and submitted this proposal, however, a minor flaw had been discovered in it. So he had quietly withdrawn the proposal, had reworked it to repair the flaw, and had then resubmitted it. Conficker B had employed the flawed proposal. Conficker C used the *revised* version. It showed once more the rare expertise of this worm's authors, and also how sedulous they were in tending their creation.

There was one piece of good news in Hassen's dissection. It was quickly realized that even though the worm generated fifty thousand new domain names every day, each bot attempted to contact only five hundred of those domains. If every one of the millions of infected computers had reached out to fifty thousand new ones every day, the volume of traffic had the potential to crash the Internet's DNS infrastructure. Initially, members of the Cabal had begun computing, or trying to compute, exactly how much traffic it would take to shut down telecommunications in North America, or to crash Google or Amazon. But much of the immediate alarm eased with this information.

Rick wrote:

So far it's not as bad as you might assume. It randomly generates a list of 50K domains but then it only tries 500 every 30 to 90 minutes. The authors realize that 50K queries would have caused issues with internal DDoS of DNS infrastructure. I suspect DNS loads will increase worldwide but the local effect should not be as bad as the worst case appears. As we get more information on how the bot works I'm sure we can estimate load more accurately.

Of course, the botnet still had the *potential* to overload the Internet's critical nodes at any time, but the Cabal had begun to sense something about their adversary. Conficker's botmaster had no interest in crashing the Internet, anymore than the worm wanted to interfere with the normal functioning of the computers it infected. It was building something to last. It *needed* the Internet.

But if there ever was a time to haul out the big guns, it had arrived. Among the long list of targeted TLDs was *.us,* the country code used by many U.S. government agencies. That ought to warrant federal attention. Rodney was head of security for Neustar, which, among other things, managed *.us,* so the feds were among its major clients. Apart from the broader public interest, Neustar had a professional obligation to inform official Washington. So on the same weekend when Phil and his Menlo Park staff were engrossed in dissecting Conficker C, Rodney flew to Washington.

He was the eldest and arguably the most heavily credentialed member of the Cabal, the one the feds might actually listen to. He was a charming man, full of rowdy energy and puckish humor, with a very understated intellect. If you ran into him in a bar you might think he worked as a trucker—and, indeed, in addition to his other skills, he *was* a trucker, owner of a Class A heavy duty commercial driver's license. Just as he was a smart man who did not behave like one, he was a rich man who didn't behave like one—although he did have one rich man's hobby: he collected and raced classic sports cars. Rodney had built himself into a major figure in the Internet world, from nothing. In South Africa as a young man he had served his mandatory tour in the army, and had then lasted only three months in college. He took a job with an insurance company, and enrolled in a course to become an actuary. The second six-month phase of the course introduced him to computers, and he had fallen in love. He took a job with Radio Shack because it offered an avenue out of South Africa, which was then ruled by an apartheid regime that Rodney found unconscionable. He began volunteering as a teacher of math and English to black adults on weekends, in a program that was not government authorized. When the regime began cracking down and arresting the students, Rodney at age twenty-two had had enough. At that point he was married and a father, and the mandatory annual tours in the army were increasingly burdensome. The brewing race war seemed to draw closer and more inevitable with each passing year, and here he was, trained and conscripted to fight on the wrong side. So he moved his family to London, and from there to Los Angeles, learning more and more with each new position about emerging global computer networks.

In addition to his day job, perhaps partly out of the habit of military service he had acquired in his home country, Rodney volunteered to work as a specialist reserve officer for the Los Angeles Police Department. When a police unit responded to a call in his Sherman Oaks neighborhood in 1983, Rodney chatted them up and discovered that among the officers in the unit were reserves who were ham radio operators—he had owned a ham radio license since 1971. They specialized in electronic snooping, which Rodney found fascinating. So he signed up. He worked two or three nights a month, usually on stakeouts in safe locations, work that freed up regular officers to kick down doors. He saw all kinds of opportunities to apply computer networks to fighting crime, and strong-armed the deputy chief for his region into letting him compile a database for local crimes on his Apple IIe, and eventually on his IBM PC. He produced daily printouts of criminal activity, which were handed to patrol officers at the beginning of each shift. This practice was successful enough to be adopted department-wide. He was then selected to be trained as a drug recognition expert, and eventually became an instructor. Later he obtained that heavy-duty commercial driver's license and drove one of the department's eighteen-wheel emergency response tractor/

trailers. He was behind the wheel of the Mobile Command Post during the 1992 riots over the Rodney King case.

All the while, Rodney was accumulating a high level of skill with computer networks, just as the Internet began to blossom. When he was ready to start his own company, he and his wife shopped for a place to finally plant roots. Was there a city in the world that wasn't threatened by race war and riots, and that didn't live under the constant threat of a giant earthquake? They were ready for some peace and quiet. They wanted a place where there were no wildfires, floods, snow, ice, or tornadoes. Rodney found that the only two spots in the country that met all those requirements were Phoenix and Las Vegas. His wife vetoed the gambling capital, so Phoenix it was. One the companies he started there handled online sales for Robert Redford's Sundance Catalogue, and another evolved into Genuity, one of the largest ISP data center operators in the world. Rodney had retired from GTE, but in his long and successful climb through the Internet-world, and perhaps harking back to his police work, he had become fascinated by security issues. He supervised security for Neustar now, and knew that a botnet the size of Conficker could, among others things, shut down the company's networks, effectively dropping telecommunications off the map in North America for a period of time. So his concern about the threat was both broad and immediate.

When he got to Washington, Rodney initially contacted a friend at the Commerce Department who worked on Critical Infrastructure Protection for the National Telecommunications and Information Administration, which advised the president of the United States on Internet issues. Rodney called his friend at home on Sunday evening, March 8, outlined what was happening, and sought his advice on how best to approach the Commerce Department about this new threat.

This was Rodney's best foot-in-the-door for the massive federal bureaucracy, because he had a legitimate duty to brief the agency. Neustar's contract for administering *.us* was with the Commerce Department. So Rodney asked for a chance to present the challenge now faced by the directory, and then, for background, told his friend all about the worm, and the new strain in particular. It was the first time the official had heard about Conficker, which was a little alarming to Rodney —but he apparently grasped its significance immediately. He said he would call right back, and less than an hour later, Rodney's phone rang.

"Can you be at the Department of Commerce tomorrow morning at eight for a briefing in the chief information officer's (CIO) office?" his friend asked. He wanted Rodney to brief a variety of officials not just about the threat to *.us,* but about Conficker as a whole.

Rodney put together a PowerPoint presentation in his hotel room that night. He had packed one white shirt for the trip, for a meeting on Tuesday at which, to his chagrin, he would feel obliged to wear a suit. He broke out the shirt early Monday morning and reported punctually to the monumental, six-story, Doric-columned, gray stone Herbert C. Hoover Office Building, a structure that has stood on the entire 1400 block of Constitution Avenue for more than seventy years as a massive symbol of prosperity, the granite fortress of American commerce.

Shortly after eight o'clock Rodney was standing before a roomful of Commerce officials. Among those in attendance that morning was an attorney with a background in Internet issues who had been working on a sixty-day review of cyber issues for the newly inaugurated President Barack Obama. As Rodney began to launch into his presentation, firing up his PowerPoint display, one of the officials asked, "Didn't we already have this briefing?"

There was momentary confusion, and alarm. One does not convene the grandly important and extremely busy pooh-bahs of American prosperity for a briefing *they have already received*. Rodney's friend had a few bad moments here. It seems that someone from the U.S. Computer Emergency Readiness Team (U.S. CERT), the agency charged with protecting federal computer systems, had met with most of this very Commerce Department crowd in the previous week for "an urgent briefing." Material from that session was hastily found and presented to Rodney, who saw, to his surprise, that last week's *urgent* briefing had concerned Conficker B, which had appeared more than two months earlier. Apparently the alarm sounded by Rick Wesson in early January in his "note from the trenches" was still getting the classic bureaucratic slo-mo treatment, inching its way from department to department. It confirmed Rodney's already poor opinion of U.S. CERT.

Well, folks, if that briefing last week scared you, and it should have, you might want to tighten your seatbelts . . . .

Rodney went ahead with his presentation about Conficker C, pointing out the seemingly insurmountable challenge the Cabal now faced in protecting the Internet. When he had finished, the room was quiet. One of the officials asked Rodney if he was free to give the same presentation at one o'clock that afternoon at FBI headquarters, where U.S. CERT held a meeting about current high-level threats every other Monday. Rodney said he would have to move some things around on his schedule, but that this sounded like the kind of occasion that warranted it. The same official then left the room, and returned moments later to confirm that he had spoken to one of the deputy U.S. CERT directors, and obtained permission for Rodney to attend.

The meeting in question was a classified briefing about cyberthreats, run by U.S. CERT Director Mischel Kwon. Usually the computer security chiefs of various vital government agencies attended. Rodney left the Hoover building and went back to his Neustar offices. He knew Kwon; he had met her on several occasions. He did not want to ambush her, or show her up, given the fact that her agency seemed so far behind on the threat. He had tried to contact her several times in the previous months, but had been ignored. Still, as a courtesy, he tried again. He sent her an email, saying that he would be seeing her at the briefing in a few hours, and quickly summarizing his presentation. He closed by offering to talk to her beforehand if she wished.

Kwon responded six minutes later.

"Rodney, I appreciate your update. I must tell you that the one o'clock meeting is for government only. The only nongovernment allowed are contractors under contract directly supporting the government. Am I to understand that you will be briefing prior to the meeting? Please do know there has been a misunderstanding."

She copied the email to a number of others, among them the deputy who had authorized Rodney's attendance.

Rodney wrote back that there had been no misunderstanding, that he had been asked to brief people at the meeting at one o'clock. He was also, in fact, a contractor directly supporting the government, but he did not wish to split hairs.

"Let me know if I should cancel coming over," he wrote.

Moments later, an email flashed on Rodney's screen from the deputy who had approved the session, mailed to him and a large number of others, including Kwon. It read, simply: "He can brief at the meeting."

Rodney was startled. After all, this was supposed to be Kwon's *deputy*. He surmised that the Commerce

Department official who had spoken to the deputy earlier must have complained about hearing of the new Conficker variant from Rodney, a civilian, a naturalized citizen with a foreign accent to boot, instead of from the agency charged with responsibility for such things. Rodney could imagine how that conversation must have gone: *You mean to tell me you jackasses have no bloody idea this is happening?* He sensed serious trouble in Kwon's kingdom—indeed, she would resign five months later.

He sent her another message:

"Hey, I really don't want to cause problems for you. Really, I apologize if I did. I wanted to give you a heads-up. You don't want me to come, let me know."

Kwon fell silent. She did not respond, nor did she attend the one o'clock meeting. Rodney walked into an enormous conference room at FBI headquarters and was led to a lectern. He faced scores of officials, none of whom he recognized except for the attorney reviewing these matters for Obama, who had been at the morning briefing at Commerce. All wore security lanyards with their plastic ID prominently displayed, a totem in Washington's security-obsessed culture, demarcating privileged access and high security clearances. But there were no names on the dangling plastic. He saw every agency acronym he had heard of—FBI, SS, DOD, FAA, FCC, DOJ, NSA, CIA—and many he had not. Curiously, no one in the room introduced him or herself. Just as with the Cabal's dealings with the feds throughout, for these people information flowed in only one direction. They get your name; you don't get theirs. Rodney had brought along a USB thumb drive with his presentation, and a laptop of his own, because he knew the government had banned the use of thumb drives the previous year—a rule dating back to the fiasco of the thumb drives in the Pentagon parking lot. But instead one of the men took the drive and plugged it right into a laptop at the lectern.

Rodney laughed.

"What?" asked the man.

"I'll get to it," said Rodney.

He gave a condensed version of the presentation he had given that morning. He saw the officials in the room exchanging startled looks and shrugs with each other—*Did you know about this? I haven't heard a thing!* He told them how the botmaster had been upping his game, outmaneuvering the Cabal for months. He did his best, as Rick had done almost two months earlier, to describe the scope of the threat. He mentioned the thumb-drive issue, an infection vector ever since Conficker B, and explained his earlier laughter—his astonishment that DHS itself had evidently ignored the widely touted ban. He had been allotted fifteen minutes for his talk, and an hour later he was still at the lectern answering questions, explaining. The concern and surprise of the officials were evident. Rodney did his best not to throw U.S. CERT under the bus . . . but he could see why Kwon had tried to head off this briefing, and then had skipped it. It was embarrassing. A small group followed him out of the room when he was finished.

Rodney asked them who they were.

"I'm from the FAA," said one.

"I hope I wasn't boring you," said Rodney.

"No. I'm on my way back to Kansas City. We have an issue."

When he got back to Neustar, there were messages from several Congressional offices, asking that he come to the Hill to brief this or that senator or representative. He went right out and bought another white shirt, because clearly he was going to have a few more reasons to dress up this week.

In the Congressional Office Building the next day, between meetings, he received a message from one of the attendees of the Monday afternoon briefing, double-checking some of the details in the PowerPoint presentation. Rodney just emailed it to him from his thumb drive. One of his assistants came to him later that day and told him he had received a phone call from a contact at U.S. CERT, asking questions about Conficker. It seems the agency had been tasked to make a presentation on the worm at the White House that day. The assistant had referred him to Rodney, and the contact had responded, "We're not allowed to talk to him." So Kwon had apparently taken umbrage at Rodney's big show. But he clearly now had the feds' attention.

"People seem to be finally getting that this is not a joke," Rodney told his assistant.

The following day he was asked to brief the staff of the Senate Select Committee on Intelligence. Because the committee's offices were off-limits to those without a high security clearance, the staff arranged to meet with Rodney in the Visitors Center of the Capitol Building, in the cafeteria. About a dozen staffers met him there in the middle of the afternoon. The cafeteria was quiet and mostly empty. They cordoned off a portion of the big room with portable dividers, and sat around a long table. Before Rodney got started, one of the staffers, a young woman, interrupted him.

"Just so you know," she said, "We probably know a whole lot more about Conficker than you do. We received a classified briefing yesterday afternoon," the woman said. "So there's probably not much more you can tell us about this."

"That's really good news," said Rodney, his voice heavy with sarcasm. By now he knew without a doubt how clueless the establishment was. The woman's arrogance annoyed him. He started collecting his notes.

"Since you have matters *completely* under control," he said, "then there's no reason for me to be wasting any more of your time."

As he stood, there was a chorus of nos.

"Stay," protested one of the staffers.

"We want to hear it," said another.

So Rodney sat back down. He took out copies of his

PowerPoint presentation, which had been printed up on Neustar stationery. He handed them out around the table. The woman who had addressed him flipped through her copy and pronounced, "Yep, this is the same presentation we saw at the classified White House briefing yesterday."

The meeting dissolved into laughter when the staffers realized that U.S. CERT had simply taken Rodney's briefing and presented it at the White House as their own work— and *classified* it, to boot! Rodney later confirmed it with his White House contact, who had attended all three of the sessions—"They just gave yours as their own," the contact said. So much for vaunted federal cyberdefenses.

This was hard work, this laboring to rouse the great slumbering giant of the U.S. government, trying to enlist its vast resources in the fight. He had been successful, to a point. That Thursday, T.J. passed along a request to add eight U.S. CERT officials to the List.

So Rodney was stung, after this weeklong uphill slog, to find himself being sniped at by some in his own ranks. No one from the Cabal itself, at least not directly, but word of Rodney's briefings in Washington had spread far and wide in the Geek Tribe, as the administrators and staffers at his briefings reached out to their own trusted sources, to their own security experts, asking: *Who is this guy? Are these things he's telling us true? Is this Conficker worm as dangerous as he says it is? If so, why haven't we heard about this from you?* And at least some received answers—no doubt in some cases covering their own ass—that this Rodney Joffe fellow . . . may . . . have . . . exaggerated the danger. After all, the worm had done nothing yet. Some were far enough out of the loop that they still clung to the grad-student-stunt theory, à la the Morris Worm, which had gone out the window with Conficker B. No one who really knew the worm was making this claim, but people on the fringes, people worried that crying wolf in Washington might give the Tribe itself a bad name, feared that their own credibility might suffer by professional association. There were suggestions that Rodney, beating his drum so loudly, might have been puffing himself up.

This was—there is no other word for it—*insulting*. Rodney was a bona fide Internet pioneer. He had practically invented the techniques of e-marketing and e-commerce, and had gone on to invent the content distribution and load balancing technology that was utilized by ISPs all over the world. He wasn't some ivory tower visionary, either; he was a successful businessman. With regard to divining where this marvelous technology was going, and assessing its strengths and its weaknesses, there were few people in the world who could match his record, who *saw the whole thing* so clearly. Who better to sound the alarm? Who better to quantify the risk?

Very early on Saturday morning, still in Washington, Rodney responded passionately and at length to his critics, posting a letter to everyone on the List. It was a forceful broadside, an argument for the importance of the effort, a defense of his own efforts in Washington, a challenge, and a rallying cry. If they were going to beat this thing, they had to stop undercutting themselves.

It led to a remarkable exchange:

Gentlemen,

Based on some off-line discussion and comments, as well as the reported discomfort of some of you on the List with my activities this week, I'd like to confront the elephant in the room. . . . The problem with Conficker is not Conficker.

Since the beginning of "the Cabal," we have all been focused on the tactical issues of responding to it. Each of us in our way, and based on our own agendas. MS [Microsoft] because the initial hole was in the OS [Operating System], as well as the fact that ongoing infections and spread occurs with Windows users. Symantec and Kaspersky because the worm is a bastard to deal with and they make software that has to deal with it. Me, and the other registry operators because it uses our resources for C&C [command and control]. Registrars because C&C domains get registered through them. ISPs because they provide the transport and their customers are affected. Researchers because they see it and analyze it. Some of us (you) play multiple roles.

But none of us has really dealt with why this is bad stuff. Conficker has been relatively harmless so far, as far as we know. And as I was asked and admitted repeatedly as I rang the bells in Washington, we have no evidence that it has [been] or will be used maliciously. Some on this list have posited that it may just be an experiment that was wildly successful, or perhaps a group of coders proving they can write good code.

I was a reserve police officer in Los Angeles for 20 years. I learned that there is real crime in the world. And that some people are just plain evil (well, I knew that from before, but only through the lessons of history—working the streets of LA gave me firsthand experience at how common it was). Working a homicide scene shows you how even 2-bit gang bangers can be truly evil given half a chance.

So I say "b*llsh*t." This isn't a game. Looking at this list, every one of you has been the victim of a 6/20/11 DDoS. You've all dealt with spam. I know that most of you have been *pwned,* and had your keystrokes logged or traffic sniffed by malware. And at least one of you has been on the receiving end of extortion. So *you* know better. You *know* what a botnet can do. A small one. . . . We all know that a botnet of Conficker's size is an effing lethal weapon in the wrong hands.

Well, who do you think the wrong hands are?

I have been accused of spreading fud in Washington. Of making a bigger thing of this than it is. So I want a discussion here and now to deal with this once and for all. Otherwise pfffffft to you. You're taking your employer's money or the taxpayer's money under false pretenses.

This is also *not* about PR. I have not had a single conversation that wasn't covered by some sort of requirement of confidentiality. The only conversations I have had are with one of you, or a government official who serves in some or other form as a specialist in security, or a legislator or staffer with TS [top security] clearance or better on a committee that has Cybersecurity under its purview. And I have not shared a single piece of information without first asking the source or author of that piece of information for permission. Period.

I have refused to allow any of our [Neustar's] employees to even take a call from the press. And I have no intention of doing so until this group reaches consensus that we need to.

Now back to the discussion.

Conficker hasn't caused any damage. It doesn't slow its hosts down. It hasn't eaten bandwidth. And it certainly hasn't caused me any load problems.

But what if it does?

What happens to the net in general if each of the infected hosts sends just one other infected host 20KB/s of traffic a second, all at the same time? Or makes just one 50KB web post every few seconds, to a mixture of Yahoo, CNN, Google, Hotmail and other well connected sites. Given the nice maps you have, most of the world's networks will collapse. Some of them just because they're in the path. I don't care who you are. Certainly all of the tier-2 networks would fall over. . . .

What would that do to the world? Not the Internet. The modern connected world? . . . How many infected hosts are there inside the Fortune 500? So what would it mean for the economy if the Fortune 500 all had their internal networks shut down for an hour? A day? A week?

Now let me ask you this; if you were the botmaster, and had a botnet of 2 million machines, how difficult would it be for *you* to bring the net worldwide to a halt?

Ahhh, you're really clueful. The best in the world at your job, but you're a good guy. And you wouldn't do that kind of thing. So who the hell do you think they are? Are all the miscreants stupid? Do you think they're all capitalists who need the net to be up so they can continue to siphon passwords, and read email, and surf porn?

And if you're so damn bright, why haven't you already managed to shut A/B down? Or C? Or Waledec. Or Torpig? Could it be because those bastards on the other side are as smart as you are? Or smarter? As we sit here now, they've managed to update a million of the A/B suckers, and you still don't know how they're doing it. *Right in front of you!* It took you apparently 2 days to even *notice*. And a week later you're still sucking wind.

AND YOU'RE THE BEST WE HAVE!

What happens if one of them wakes up in a bad mood tomorrow morning? Or after a night of drinking or dope or being beaten in some humongous online game decides that the rest of the world is filled with evil by their way of thinking and needs to be destroyed. Just like in the game?

So as I said in my first heated briefing on Monday, this *isn't* about Conficker. A, B, or C. Or Storm. Or Slammer. Or Torpig. Its about all of them. Those in the past, and those in the future. It's about the one evil bastard who decides that he is going to use his botnet, or a piece of it, to punish someone else. Its about the fact that the ability to use it maliciously exists. And *we* have stood by and let it happen. And we haven't marshaled all of our resources to try and deal with it. The people I talked to in Washington who make the laws and rules, and run our lives, and who we elected, and who swear to serve us—"we, the people"—have NO F**KING CLUE that this is out there. Now a few of them do, in terms that they understand. We need "them" to understand because we need "them" to give us help and resources.

Except that some of you (or your employers) are telling them that it's not that dire, or as bad as I say it is.

Tell me we're not one command away from a catastrophe. I dare you.

A few hours later, out in San Francisco, the ever-dour Paul Vixie took up the challenge, beginning with an answer to Rodney's dare, and proceeding to a broad, measured reflection on the fragility of our emerging digital world:

I won't. But I will provide some personal context, much of which is probably shared by others in this community.

These problems have been here so long that the only way I've been able to function at all is by learning to ignore them. Else I would be in a constant state of panic, unable to think or act constructively. We have been one command away from catastrophe for a long time now. . . . In a thousand small ways that I'm aware of, and an expected million other ways I'm not aware of, the world has gotten dangerous and fragile and interdependent. And that's without us even talking about power grids or the food stocks available in high population areas if rail and truck stops working for a week. AND, in a hundred large ways that I'm aware of and an expected thousand I don't know of, ethically incompatible people out in the world have acquired and will acquire assets that are lethal to the industrial world's way of life—criminals and terrorists using the Internet for asymmetric warfare is the great fear of our age, or at least it's my great fear. But I've lived with it so long that I have lost the ability to panic about it. One day at a time, I do what I can.

I do NOT want this to be interpreted by ANYONE as me disagreeing with rjoffe's basic observations and predictions. I'm saying the problem is far worse than he made it out to be. Because I am not the only one who has had to learn how to tune out the constant state of danger and get on with my life. All of us have. A full accounting of the problems we are collectively deliberately not thinking about in order to stay sane would be quite a SHOCK to any of us who saw it.

Now if people in DC have been telling other people in DC that there's no emergency here in Internet-land, and that they've got it all under control, then they are certainly wrong, but as to whether they're ignorant and confused, or self-serving liars, I could not say from what little I know.

But if people in DC are telling other people in DC that this is not the same threat level as 9/11, then they've probably got a point. Tomorrow the Internet MAY die for several days, if some botherder gets jilted by a boyfriend or whatever. There WOULD be loss of life and whole lot of money as a result. But there'd be no way to politicize it the way that 9/11 was politicized, because not all the fire trucks and ambulances would be in the same place or shown on the same nightly news program. So from a DC denizen's point of view, the Internet's not in trouble, by the odd definition of "trouble" that most DC denizens have to use. And we all ought to be worried about a world that's as broken as all that.

I don't advocate that we learn to live with this new class of threat, but I also don't know what choices we have. In a free world it will be possible for this kind of thing to happen.

We need more vigilance and more objective measurements; we need to change some fundamentals so that LE [law enforcement] can track these guys down in any country they operate from and kick in their doors and haul them away in chains and haul their computers away in trucks. We need a LOT of help from government, and we CANNOT be telling people in government that we've got it under control because we absolutely DO NOT HAVE IT UNDER CONTROL. At best we have it under light surveillance in-between the times one of us goes out on a donut break.

It was a dark vision of where things were heading, but a legitimate one. C-Day was just eight days away.

10

CYBARMAGEDDON

AND IS IT ANY LESS MAD TO BELIEVE A
HANDFUL OF MUTANTS MIGHT SAVE THE ENTIRE
WORLD?
—The Amazing X-Men

John Crain had been minding his own business, literally, that evening at the Holiday Inn in Atlanta in early February at the Georgia Tech DNS symposium when his boss volunteered him to save the Internet from Conficker.

His official title at ICANN was so complex that he would just tell people, "It's very long and it has something to do with security," and then hand them his card. Since the Georgia Tech conference had been convened to compare notes and discuss all the ways the Internet was at risk, it made sense for him to attend. Security issues had not been paramount when ICANN was established in 1998, taking over the role of assigning and keeping track of domain names and numbers worldwide. But as the malware problem grew in intensity and sophistication, its position as the only international body with any slight authority over the Internet had turned John's security job into a pivotal one. The Georgia Tech conference was an effort to draw together the disparate players concerned about the threat, and John had helped set it up. He had been roped into attending the Cabal's rump session that night by ICANN's president, Paul Twomey.

And when his boss turned to him to be ICANN's point man with the Cabal, John said the only thing a man who loves his job can say in such circumstances: *Yes, sir . . . now . . . what exactly are we talking about here?*

The specific task that night was to get China on board, since the newly released B strain included that country's TLD (*.cn*), and because most of the infected computers were there, and because nobody else in the room had a clue as to how to go about enlisting the help of the Middle Kingdom—Rick Wesson having not yet informed the group about his own outreach to China. Perhaps because of Rick's unauthorized outreach, the task happily proved to be a lot easier than anyone, including John, imagined. A few phone calls and a couple of emails.

Still, John had earned a reputation for working wonders, so when Conficker C upped the ante from 250 to fifty thousand domains, and the list of eight targeted TLDs to 116, all eyes again turned his way. He made a terrific ambassador, easy to talk to, fun, the kind of guy who loves to sip good whiskey and talk music. John projects no hint of his profound—really, one-of-a-kind—level of international expertise. The Internet is so new that even those capable of doing John's job could not have accumulated his contacts and experience.

He has a broad face with a small, pinched mouth and prominent, dark arching eyebrows, with straight dark hair that forms a striking widow's peak. He combs it straight back, in a style that, with the eyebrows, can give him a slightly diabolical look, which is misleading, because he is both cheerful and unfailingly straightforward. He had somehow contracted a passion while growing up in the East Midlands of England, in Leicester, for 1950's-era American country and rockabilly music. Long before he even contemplated moving to the United States he had begun affecting cowboy boots and shirts—his friends called him "Tex." At about the same time he had begun working with computers, playing video games like *Star Trek* with his brother and father, and tapping into the mainframe of British Gas, where his father worked. In the three decades since—he was now forty-three—he had earned a degree in mechanical engineering and had set to work on computer networks when the Internet was still in its infancy. Dressed now in somewhat fancier cowboy boots and shirts, John has become the globe-trotting *something-to-do-with-security* man for ICANN, working when he is not on the road from an alcove in a spare bedroom of his suburban home in Long Beach, California, where he settled in search of perfect weather—"I was working with this American fellow in Amsterdam, and it was raining, and he said, 'Why don't you come to California? It's not raining there.'"

When Conficker C arrived, John had three weeks to enlist the help of nearly a third of the TLDs in the world, including every top-level country code. If a nation had its own TLD, John had to recruit it to play ball with the Cabal. This meant asking the Domain Name Server (DNS) in countries on every continent . . . well, the pitch might have gone something like this:

Kind sir, with apologies, would you mind terribly setting aside this long list of domains? (Since the servers made money for every domain name they sold, this was asking them to essentially give away hundreds or perhaps eventually thousands of revenue-generating items.) And would you also set up a system to intercept inquiries sent to these domain names by this nasty botnet Conficker beginning on April 1, and redirect them all to a sinkhole operated by this grad student named Chris Lee at an American university in Atlanta, Georgia, called Georgia Tech—you know, "The Ramblin' Wreck"? Everybody over here has heard of it. Really. In doing so, kind sir, you will be performing a heroic service to the health of the Internet, and, need I mention, for the reputation of your registry and country. (Just think how bad you are going to look if you don't play along!) . . . And (forget about getting any credit for your generosity here) would you mind keeping this all secret? We'll supply you with the lists, trust us . . . and . . . and . . . oh yes, if any of those randomly generated domains happens to be owned already, for every "collision," we'll be needing you to authenticate its ownership and then contact the poor sap and work out arrangements to shut him down . . . but only for a few days! . . . in order to protect him from being swamped by the evil botmaster . . . and . . . did I forget to mention? . . . just one more little thing . . . would you please do this every day for . . . ever? From now until the end of time?

Okay. It sure didn't sound like an easy sell. Some members of the Cabal had concerns about even making the pitch. What if this country-by-country effort succeeded, and then resulted in breaking a law somewhere, or prompted some TLD, acting at the Cabal's behest, to anger one of the website owners whose domain "collided" with Conficker's daily list?

"I do not have to want to avoid travel to certain parts of the world because 'XX' years ago I tried to help the Internet, and someone felt I violated some privacy law and filed a suit which resulted in a warrant for my arrest in YY country," wrote Dre Ludwig.

The botmaster was, of course, counting on this being an impossible sell, and John had little quarrel with that logic. He expected to fail. It was his job . . . but . . . are you serious? *Really?* Remember, ICANN has no authority whatsoever. There are no little black helicopters to swoop in and enforce the global will. There is no applicable international law.

And who could even characterize this as the *global* will? This was coming from an ad hoc group of volunteers—the X-Men!—with no official role even in the United States, much less in the world community. Chris Lee was still in grad school, for Chrissake! (He did, however, already have a PhD.) Few of the people running these things—in Africa? in South America? in Asia?—had ever heard of Conficker, much less of the Cabal. ICANN had no leverage beyond an appeal to international fellowship and John Crain's charm. And yet . . . wasn't it in everyone's interest to keep the Internet functioning smoothly? The global network rested upon a common commitment to good sense and goodwill. Didn't it?

Some of the TLDs involved began asking why Microsoft wasn't just buying up all of the Conficker-generated domains itself. After all, it was Microsoft's leaky software that allowed the worm to flourish, and everybody had been reading for years about Bill Gates's countless billions. This touched upon widespread resentment of the giant software company for owning such a huge share of the market worldwide, and in some cases for corporate practices considered predatory. Some of this discussion found its way to the List, where T.J. remained conspicuously silent on the subject. When one of the TLD operators complained that Microsoft should have to pay for "cleaning up its own mess," Paul Vixie responded with frustration:

Then perhaps you should organize a class action lawsuit. But it's not in scope for the public health crisis to wonder what company profited from creating the fragile conditions. (or else the board and CEO of McDonald's would be in prison for the world's diabetes problems.) We REALLY digress.

Even Paul, who shared this view of Microsoft's responsibility, could see the folly of assigning blame while the Internet was . . . *on fire!*

The Cabal set upon working out various technological solutions, some way of automating the process of blacklisting or blocking the never-ending list of potential command locations. How better to fight a computer than with a computer? But the problem was less technical than political. In order to put an automated process to work, they would still need the full cooperation of every one of those TLDs. The biggest problem was collisions. In these cases the owners of the sites had to be checked out and enlisted in the effort, and if even one balked, if even one was owned by or paid off by the botmaster, the whole effort could fail. The authors of the worm had already managed to upgrade it twice by registering several domains right under their noses.

John began shipping off the "ask" in mid-March. In those cases where there were collisions, Chris Lee would contact the unlucky website operator directly with the request to block traffic on the given date and instructions on how to direct it to his sinkhole.

Needless to say, this was a strange note to get. Unprecedented. Some noodle you never heard of in Atlanta, Georgia, U.S.A., writes to you out of the blue and asks you, for the good of humanity, to shut down your business for a day and reroute all your web traffic to him! One contractor, who managed a website that collided with the worm's list, happened to be a Georgia Tech grad himself, so he wrote back to Chris:

> I believe that this email is not from you, nor is it in your general character, to send out such an email. But if somebody is sending out this email, with the "From" address spoofed to your name, thought you might like to know. Also, perhaps, you can help me solve the riddle of what the "real" intent or endgame of this email is. Technically speaking . . . it is clear that this is a hoax . . . [I cannot imagine you] sitting at home psycho-obsessively finding/predicting secret lists of likely Conficker victim domains, researching all their whois records, and writing to every one of these 500 people in need of YOUR rescue, per day . . . hmm.

This was, of course, very nearly what the Cabal was doing, except that relatively few of the domain names generated by the worm actually belonged to anyone. Chris forwarded the note to Rodney, who promptly boomed a warning shot across the contractor's bow that opened with a weighty recitation of his credentials—senior vice president and senior technologist of Neustar, member of

the ICANN Security and Stability Advisory Committee—
and then explained that, improbable as it might seem,
"The Conficker binary does, as Dr. Lee noted, generate
500 random domain names each day that it then uses to
contact the Conficker C&C [command and control]. The
algorithm has been decoded, and so we know in advance
what domain names will be used by the C&C and bots every
day from now on, subject to the malware being updated."
Rodney continued:

> Dr. Lee, and others in this core group, have compared
> the domain names that are due to be used by the C&C
> with domains that are already registered. Obviously the
> randomness of the malware algorithm results in some collisions
> with domains that have already been registered. Your client's
> domain name is one of those very few. The unregistered
> domains have been dealt [with] . . . but the concerns are for
> those few domains like your client's that will now receive millions
> of connections from compromised Conficker systems on their
> "magical" day—in your client's case, March 18th. And in order
> for the Conficker authors to successfully operate, their best bet
> is to compromise the machines behind your client's domain
> name by March 18th. Hence Dr. Lee's concern, and his email to
> you. Please be assured, unfortunately, that the people behind
> Conficker are highly sophisticated in their ability to compromise
> web servers, even those that are especially hardened. So I
> would urge you to heed Dr. Lee's offer of help. Despite what
> you may believe based on looking at his public pages at GT
> [Georgia Tech], he is an expert in this field, and one of our best.

That got the bastard in line.

Stephane Bortzmayer, who worked for Association Française pour le Nommage Internet en Coopération (AFNIC), a targeted French registry, was irritated by John's request:

> I am a simple employee and have zero authority to decide what AFNIC will or will not do. The letter . . . reads as if the decision has already been taken. It even seems to contain threats to non-compliers. . . . Same thing when you ask people, not to discuss the actions to take, but to simply report what stage they are in, in the implementation of an already-decided plan. I suggest that we first discuss the solution (is blocking thousands of domains a scalable solution, when Conficker can always extend its list?). It does not seem that there is, for Conficker C, a published implementation of the algorithm. Therefore, we have to blindly trust the list of domain names. That's annoying.

John wrote back to apologize for any confusion, and pointed out that the letter he had sent was, in fact, just a request. Rick Wesson also responded:

> Please understand that there is some urgency and the task to even attempt a global response coordination within 18 days is difficult. As far as decision making, each TLD has made their own decision. The effort only works if we *all* decide it is in the global interest to participate. This is the decision most organizations are taking.

Rick sent him the link and a password to the List, so he could verify the nature of the effort for himself. Stephane came on board, but only after asking for and receiving a cover-your-ass document with a certified signature, which was a little strange, there being no real authority in a position to give an order or make a demand.

The strain of getting this done with the clock ticking relentlessly showed within the Cabal. The List, previously calm and professional in tone for the most part, usually deep into the technical issues of sinkholing and tracking a multimillion-node botnet, but also eloquent on occasion, degenerated in some predictable quarters, and also in some less predictable ones.

The sheer volume of data being accumulated by all the domains Conficker C was programmed to generate required that the sinkholing operation be expanded. This was just one of the complications the botmaster apparently hoped would unravel the Cabal. It did not, but it definitely added stress.

Rick kicked up a row inadvertently when he breezily volunteered his company to do some of the work:

> I expect to play a role with sinkholing C just cuz I got a /16 [a very large Internet interface] to play with and it sounds fun.

His tone rubbed Paul Vixie the wrong way.

That's not a good reason, especially for a key man who is already carrying a large coordination burden for the overall project. . . . I am aggravated by your use of the words "play" and "fun." This is a deeply serious activity on which we have collectively and individually screwed every possible pooch there was to screw in the A/B effort [Conficker A and B]."

Rick wasn't giving up.

It's all in how you look at your job. I heard a One Star [General] refer to tanks as toys and Browning M2s as popguns. I guess it comes from scale and your individual reference. I still enjoy my job =) so yes, even really serious stuff to you still seems like fun and a good time to me. I'd rather have an interesting day job than, well, deal with drama like this.

He went on to complain about various technical issues relating to the sharing of sinkholed data, and suggested that Paul was being held to a different, less stringent standard. Paul wrote back to defend himself, telling Rick to stop comparing their operations, and reminding him that while he, Paul, had never accused Rick of sharing data inappropriately, he still wasn't ruling out the possibility that he had (and had lied about it):

If you've been sharing data with people who the rest of us don't know about, then that's a problem, and if you haven't, then it's not a problem.

Rick responded:

> I hated high school for the same reasons this thread
> exists. If there is anything that makes me never want to do this
> again, it's working on projects until they digress into he said/
> she said. It's happened more than once with you, Paul. I'll not
> be participating in this thread any longer. If you have an issue
> you need to discuss with me, pick up the phone.

The matter would have ended there, except that Rick's accusation, that Paul had also allowed unauthorized access to sinkholed Conficker data, inadvertently implicated another key member of the Cabal, Chris Lee, who was now managing the bulk of the sinkhole operation. Ordinarily a very mild, detail-oriented, unemotional technician, Chris finally unloaded on the most feisty and (some felt) fishy member of the group, bringing up his still-simmering indignation over Rick's rogue approach to China:

> When I operate the sinkhole, I wear my GT [Georgia Tech]
> hat. In this case, there existed a clandestine exfiltration of that
> data to another country—one that is well-known to leverage
> cyber-capabilities, which created a direct conflict of interest
> with my activities and my employer. You knew this and did
> not tell me or anyone else. I collected data in a very open
> fashion, . . . and with the impression that the data was only
> being shared within the Cabal. When I addressed my concern
> to you, you treated me as if I were trying to undermine the
> entire effort and gave veiled threats. There were plenty of

opportunities for you to clearly state your motives to me and work out a nice compromise, but that's not the route you chose at the time.

Now I cannot trust you. This undermines our entire effort. You don't trust me and everything I do or say (or even silence), you view as an attack or "a game." This will not work. We either work out our differences, or at least one of us will have to leave. I hope that I'm humble enough to continue to listen, understand, and find good solutions, but that window is closing fast as I am starting to feel attacked and am losing my objectivity. Your other activities of talking with various government organizations, NYT [the *New York Times*], and to the cc TLD without coordination and oversight also expands my suspicion of your activities. You seem to want to avoid any checks on your actions and try to hide what you're doing. This cannot scale. We are a team. We have the same goals (roughly). We can work this out.

I have been silent recently, in hopes that my objections would not stand in the way of all of us working together and to avoid everything I say from sounding like an attack or being attacked by someone who is suspicious of me. We are at the cusp of doing great things together, let's stop the games (as Joffe has yelled clearly in email) and work together. I am not attacking you and I do not think you are evil. We do have a difference in approach and opinion—one that could easily be solved. I think you are avoiding oversight because you think some of us will be hostile toward you and attack. This is likely not the case. Hiding what you do will cause animosity.

We were friends once, Rick. I want to be friends again.

The three eventually retreated to hammering out their differences on the telephone, but not until after Rick once more posted a reference to their contretemps as a "high school drama." Chris complained about the analogy, prompting Dre Ludwig to weigh in and address Rick directly:

> It is my humble estimation that you are out of line with not only your response, but multiple actions you have taken over the last month and a half. I agree with all of Chris's previous points and there are serious trust issues that you have caused yourself. I think every individual [who] is a part of this effort has a legitimate right to ask questions of you based on what you have already told this group. You may not understand it but the circles you are trying to swim in are rather small but very deep. Any ripple that is made has a tendency to reflect off of multiple individuals in this group.

Dre complained that Rick had still never supplied a list of everyone with whom he had shared the sinkhole data.

> Let me also restate one thing. Rick, this is not a personal attack. If it was such there would be NO ROOM for misinterpretation on my part. We need cold hard facts not personal attacks, misdirection, or lack of results. I had asked for this on previous phone calls and I have yet to see anything come of it. So please let us avoid the "high school drama" as you put it, and deal with cold hard data.

Their dispute then vanished from the List, as they worked the dispute out on the phone, but animosity and suspicion remained. On March 24, just a week before C-Day, Rick posted an angry note to Paul, who had complained that the effort was flagging and that some sinkhole operators might need to be replaced:

> I am growing tired of you stating that "it is not working." It is but you are just unsatisfied in how it is working. Be clear, post some statistics, or shut up. You don't get to remove any A/B [Conficker A and B] sinkhole operators, but I can remove you. So pipe down.

Paul responded . . . .

Finally, T. J. Campana, up in his office in the Redmond sprocket, had had enough. He wrote:

> STOP . . . What hurts the efforts the MOST is the bullshit that is being tossed around here. Either we learn to play nice or we (meaning I) will make arrangements for both of you to go home. We need to do better, but this will not happen overnight. For some of us, this is our first stab at sinkholing a threat and we are having some growing pains.

Rodney wasn't far behind, once more stepping up as the "adult in the room":

> CUT THE BULLSHIT INFIGHTING OUT!

Don't you realize that from the outside (and maybe in reality) the cohesive group that has worked so well to get us this far is about to fall apart.

NONE of you will win. The only winner[s] will be the people we're fighting to defeat. I guarantee that if we don't get our shit together, the next NYT [*New York Times*] or WP [*Washington Post*] headline will be "Conficker Cabal Collapses." And I don't want to be part of that.

So please recognize that every time one of you pisses on another's shoes, hundreds of people are seeing it, one way or the other.

When I organized the group meeting in Atlanta, my objective was to help find a solution to one part of the problem, with the hope that it would help to find a way to survive against the bad guys. That is still my prime objective. Unlike some of you, I don't have a business model that is part of the Conficker battle. I don't sell software that deals with Conficker. I don't sell services that deal with Conficker. I don't sell hardware that deals with Conficker. I don't have a consulting business that deals with Conficker. I am just an Internet user, with a little bit of history and a few thousand customers. And I want the Internet to survive.

If there are any of you on this list that feel differently, then say so and let those of us with a different primary objective go somewhere else to continue the fight.

Otherwise, please get together, and make some decisions that work for all of us, and ultimately for the Internet.

I still suggest a group call to work things out and reestablish a united front. I don't want to get any more calls from people on one of the lists asking me wtf is going on with the "leaders."

And even if you continue to ignore my "public" requests for answers, please at least acknowledge that you got this email, and have an interest in solving the problem.

T.J. called for another phone conference, wherein all parties agreed to behave.

The countdown to C-Day continued.

John and Rick made a little wager on who could get the most TLDs enlisted—a thirty-year-old bottle of Glenfiddich Scotch. It was no contest. John ended up securing commitments from one hundred of the TLDs himself; Rick corralled the other sixteen. By the end of March, they had done the impossible. Poland had certain legal constraints; its registry could not by law set aside the projected domain names without being paid, and since there was no time to change the law. Rick pulled out his own credit card again.

The results amazed the Cabal; they had done it! The botmaster had challenged them to do the impossible, and they had done so.

John was more amazed than anyone else. The request was outrageous, and . . . yet . . . everybody said yes. Every one. Some took a little longer than others, but eventually they *all* signed on. The response improved his estimation of human nature, not to mention his liquor cabinet.

Rodney waxed Churchillian, calling it "our finest hour."

Still, none of them was cocky enough to believe that

when April 1 rolled around, the worm would be completely contained. There was the peer-to-peer issue to consider. Even if every last one of the possible domains was tied down to Chris Lee's sinkhole, the bots could theoretically bypass the web lookups altogether and update themselves directly. So the cloud still hovered.

And the rest of the world was suddenly, as the clock approached C-Day, waking up to Conficker . . . *way up*. The effort now included hundreds of eager geeks worldwide laboring in subgroups of the Cabal. Knowledge of the effort had spread farther still, with all those government agency staffers Rodney and others had been beseeching for weeks. With so many people engaged and interested, the story started showing up everywhere, well beyond the prescribed borders of the cybersecurity trade blogs. Only, as it traveled, the message got distorted.

It grew. *And grew*. In mid-March, as the countdown moved toward single digits, alarms began to sound in the wider world. This enormous botnet was programmed to call home and get instructions on April 1, and *nobody knew* what was going to happen. A dedicated team of experts had been working around the clock for months to stop it, but there was no guarantee they would succeed. It was as good as the plot of a Hollywood thriller. Was the Internet going to explode? Would e-commerce grind to a halt? The vital computer networks governing the nation's electrical grid, air traffic control, transit systems, telecommunications . . . were they going to fly off the rails? Would there be vast theft? Targeted takedowns? Cascading failures?

Again it was John Markoff at the *New York Times* who started things off, the first of the mainstream reporters to weigh in, just as he had reported first on the Morris Worm two decades earlier. Markoff had dinner with Rick in San Francisco, and his update on the Conficker threat ran a few days later, on March 19, under the entirely sensible headline, "Computer Experts Unite to Hunt Worm."

"An extraordinary behind-the-scenes struggle is taking place between computer security groups around the world and the brazen author of a malicious software program called Conficker," his story began.

He summarized the global nature of the threat, pointing out that the worm had built a botnet to match any in history, and referred to the struggle as "a cat-and-mouse game" that the Cabal was in danger of losing. He noted the government's apparent lack of knowledge or interest. Typically, it was Rick who furnished the punchiest quote:

"I walked up to a three-star general on Wednesday and asked him if he could help me deal with a million-node botnet. I didn't get an answer."

"An examination of the [Conficker] program reveals that the zombie computers are programmed to try to contact a control system for instructions on April 1," Markoff wrote. "There has been a range of speculation about the nature of the threat posed by the botnet, from a wake-up call to a devastating attack."

Phil Porras told the reporter, "Perhaps the most obvious frightening aspect of Conficker C is its clear potential to do harm. Perhaps in the best case, Conficker may be used as a sustained and profitable platform for massive Internet fraud and theft. In the worst case, Conficker could be turned into a powerful offensive weapon for performing concerted information warfare attacks that could disrupt not just countries, but the Internet itself."

The account was entirely responsible and accurate, but you don't run a story in the *New York Times* using terms like "zombie computers" and "devastating attack" and "frightening" without stirring things up.

Holy shit! Within days the Cabal's problem was no longer getting people to pay attention. Now it was trying to dampen what amounted to end-time hysteria—*Cybarmageddon!*—at least in certain circles of the press. The truth is that there was something predictable in these amplified alarms, an edge of . . . what to call it? Sarcasm. Sarcasm had crept in, and it was . . . frankly, annoying. Even insulting. The public relishes few things more exorbitantly than a good doomsday prediction. At least, the ones more apt to prompt a chuckle, as opposed, say, to something remotely real enough to get folks stocking the backyard bomb shelter. This particular cataclysm seemed safely confined to the netherworld of cyberspace. There was no need to hoard canned goods, store water, load the shotguns, or assume the crash position.

This was some sort of a *virtual* apocalypse, a meltdown out there in the parallel universe of incomprehensible computer systems, and . . . face it, not everybody was in love with his computer or the Internet anyway. So what if it had the geeks riled up? Remember Y2K? Predictions of worldwide collapse when the clock ticked over from December 31, 1999, to January 1, 2000? "Chaos 2000" painted in jubilant scrawls on highway overpasses? Despite the fondest hopes of doomsday-lovers everywhere, night had passed into day, the cocks had crowed, New Year revelers had awakened hungover, rubbed the sleep from their eyes, and life had resumed its normal petty pace. Besides, there was a healthy portion of the population who actually remembered the pre-digital age, who recalled that life had hummed along just fine and, if truth be told, *at a normal speed* . . . a more pleasant speed, before anyone had ever even heard of an iPhone. Remember the days when, if you had a problem with your phone, all you had to do was call Ma Bell, and a *person* answered, and a nice man came right out and gave you a new one, for free? Losing all this Internet crap didn't sound like the end of the world to *lots* of people. So these reports of a pending *Cybarmageddon!* began coming with a noticeable wink. Call it the Y2K wink. Conficker even made David Letterman's monologue—his comical announcer Alan Kalter called it "Con-*flick*er" and warned the *Late Show* audience to brace itself for a pending catastrophe: the thing had remotely turned on the webcam of Dave's computer . . . and captured him nude . . . and . . . *the pictures will be coming soon to the Internet!*

The worm was becoming a punch line. It had a hint of the *we're-getting-our-comeuppance-here* appeal of the old *Godzilla* movies. Only this wasn't a fire-breathing dragon emerging from the depths to exact revenge on mankind for having the temerity to split the atom: it was Big Brother; it was HAL; it was the long-awaited, long-predicted confrontation with The Machine, the incomprehensible monster with a billion arms that we had foolishly entrusted with all of the details of our personal and public lives . . . only . . . it really probably wasn't. Who schedules Armageddon for April Fools' Day, anyway? This was a billion-armed digital monster with a sense of humor!

On the last night of March, C-Day eve, CBS TV weighed in on *60 Minutes,* the most watched and most respected news program on the tube. The network had good reason to take Conficker seriously, its own computer network had been invaded by the worm. So CBS TV played it straight. After going to considerable expense and effort to scrub its networks, Murrow's old channel found the worm no laughing matter.

But there was still the Y2K wink.

Correspondent Leslie Stahl reported soberly, telling millions of viewers, "The Internet is infected." The story worked primarily as a warning against all forms of "creepy, crawly toxic software"—again, the wink! The segment was a terrific advertisement for commercial security firms, particularly Symantec, whose vice president Steve Trilling cheerfully explained the botnet thus: "Imagine a network of spies that has infiltrated a country. And every day, all of the spies are calling in for their instructions on what to do next."

Stahl said, "So far, the bad guys who created it haven't triggered Conficker. It's just sitting out there like a sleeper cell." Ever since 9/11, few Americans didn't sit up straight in their living rooms at the talk of "sleeper cells." But these malevolent terrorists were lurking right inside their home computer, perhaps right there *on . . . their . . . lap!* When Stahl asked what the worm might do, Trilling answered, "That's the interesting thing. The only thing the worm is being asked to do is to ask for further instructions."

The worm could turn menacing "in an instant," Stahl explained, and added, "I'm hearing *Jaws* music."

There it was again: the w*ink!*

She wrapped up the report with:

"Conficker investigators have been talking about an April Fool's attack . . . but nobody knows if the instructions will be benign, or something that could disrupt the entire Internet."

So, there you had it. If you understood the risk and chose to actually think about it (the very thing Paul Vixie had said he consciously avoided doing), and if you followed the potential risks to where they might lead, there was more than a small chance that the word *Cybarmageddon* was entirely justified. *Hey, what if this was really it?*

The Cabal had succeeded big-time in one way: They had publicized the hell out of the worm. They had come a long way from their initial press release in early January, which got mentioned in a few cybersecurity blogs. Now it was:

"An Unthinable Disaster in the Making!"—*New York Times.*

"A Threat That Could Disrupt the Entire Internet!"— *60 Minutes.*

"A Deadly Threat!"—*London Guardian.*

This alarm was being amplified and interpreted by countless smaller news outlets throughout the world, but nearly always with . . . the *wink.*

All of this made the Cabal very uneasy; their reaction was not unlike the sensations they had felt when Rodney toured the capital beating the botnet drum. One of the great risks in pushing the global panic button is, of course, making a fool of yourself. They had wanted to be taken seriously, but this hardly qualified. This was . . . like . . . *virtual* panic. The public was not so much alarmed as *amused.* What the hell was going on?

The problem was the nature of the thing. The threat was *all potential.* If you told people that there was a dirty bomb in Times Square, they would understand immediately. But to grasp the threat posed by Conficker, you had to understand how the Internet worked, how vital it had become to modern society, and how much damage someone could do with millions of computers all pulling at the same time on the same rope.

Rodney had his own little prayer for the moment: "Please, God, let it be an experiment that's gone wildly right."

So a million eyes were watching and waiting when the atomic clocks that calculate Coordinated Universal Time ticked off the final seconds of March 2009, edging toward C-Day, the moment when the C strain would receive its instructions, when the mighty botnet would wake up . . .

and!!!

and!!!

!!!

!!

!

. . . nothing happened.

11

APRIL FOOLS

X-MEN, OUR DAY HAS COME.

—The X-Men Chronicles

History is done with Appomattox moments. Wars no longer end in ways anyone can describe as satisfactory, much less triumphant. In modern warfare there is no such thing as unqualified victory, or unconditional defeat. No more Lee handing over his sword, no more Shigemitsu scratching out his signature on the deck of the USS *Missouri* with newsreel cameras capturing the moment of total surrender, with people dancing in Times Square, kissing strangers. Modern wars peter out. Casualties mount. The public gets surly. The treasury coffers bottom out. The ruling party gets dumped. One no longer wins; one *claims victory*. Often both sides do. And sometimes both are right . . . in their own way.

Another signature feature of modern war: perception

is paramount! In that category, Conficker was definitely a bust. A joke.

Lampooning the disaster warnings, a website devoted to malware research, MW-Blog, invoked the breakthrough, strange-loop moment from Hofstadter's *Gödel, Escher, Bach* when a complex recursive program *pops out* of the system, blinks, and starts thinking for itself:

> This is what security experts around the world have feared for a long time. The Conficker worm botnet grew big enough and 1 minute past midnight, on April 1st, it finally gained consciousness. News is rolling in from New Zealand that a photo frame with embedded XP went crazy and started displaying pictures of dirty deeds, done with sheep.

The Cabal took it on the chin. The geeks had cried wolf! Again!

Wired magazine poked fun that morning on its website, in a clever blog written by Kevin Poulsen:

> We'll track this scourge throughout the day, so check back frequently for the latest updates. The war room will live-blog the cyber apocalypse until the Internet has melted into a smoldering pile of solder and CAT 5 cable, or Conficker-controlled androids burst down our doors and pry our keyboards from our hands.
>
> Obviously, it's biding its time—lulling us into a false sense of security and planning its next move. Keep watching this page.

> . . . **12:20 EDT**: Reader reports, "I just got a message that said, 'Windows has encountered a problem and will need to shut down.' OMG!!"
>
> . . . **4:30 p.m. EDT:** First "I Survived Conficker" tee spotted on Cafe Press. Premature and smug. Might as well wear a sign on your chest saying, "Conficker, Kill Me First."

You get the picture. And this was the friendly, geek press. To the wider world, Conficker was just another doomsday moment that fizzled, and another reason to take the frantic warnings of the Tribe with a grain of salt.

But the prospect that nothing would happen on April 1 had actually become the prevailing theory of the Cabal itself. The insight that Conficker's botmaster had no interest in crashing the Internet had eased concern weeks earlier over the possibility of anything catastrophic. The whole point of the botnet, at least so far as anyone could tell, was to build a stable, functional infrastructure, a platform, something its creators could use whenever they wished—to sling spam, to pilfer data, maybe even to launch a cyberattack. But the Cabal would discover that once you let loose an idea as fun as a global cybermeltdown, there is no taking it back.

Some of the more sober publications had done their best. The *Wall Street Journal* had posted its verdict on its economics website:

"The truth is that the threat posed by Conficker is almost entirely theoretical, and that only a handful of dedicated professionals will notice anything out of the ordinary when

[C-Day] comes around."

The *WSJ* blog quoted Phil Porras, exactly the right person to ask.

"I don't see anything on April 1st that will cause any significant havoc," he said. "The most likely outcome is that the day will pass and no one will have noticed anything."

John Markoff of the *New York Times* had asked if he could hang around Phil's office on April 1, and Phil told him yes, but added that he would probably be bored, warning, "Nothing's likely to happen." The *Today Show* had invited Phil to come on C-Day morning, but he had declined. He hung around his Menlo Park office instead, keeping his eye on his digital ranch and on the List, tending to other things. Markoff didn't come.

Three hours after the UTC [Coordinated Universal Time] clock ticked into April, T. J. Campana wryly posted:

So we are three hours into the event and I wanted to have a status check. . . . We saw a dip in our sinkhole telemetry this evening at MS [Microsoft] . . . but there are a number of factors at play that could have caused that. The Internet still works . . . :-)

In fact, *something* had happened. The worm did exactly what it was programmed to do. The requests for instruction came knocking, by the millions, from all of the bots scattered all over the world, to each of the five hundred domains generated for that day, and all of them appeared to have been shunted toward the sinkhole at Georgia Tech, just as John Crain and Rick Wesson and the others had arranged.

Was this victory?

They wouldn't know for certain for at least a few days if they had blocked every potential command location; and, of course, even if they had, they would have to be perfect again tomorrow, and the next day, and the next, and every day thereafter— but that was unlikely. April 1 was just the first day it would be possible for the botmaster to issue a command. The Cabal had mounted a historic, truly heroic effort to prevent such commands, but only time would tell whether the botnet was fully contained. And with all the publicity they had generated, with everybody in the world watching, wouldn't C-Day be the *least likely day* for the bad guys to make their move? Given the superb gamesmanship they had demonstrated so far, wouldn't it make more sense for them to let all the hype just go pfffft? Send the X-Men a giant raspberry?

Rodney Joffe felt it. He grew increasingly incensed throughout the day with the silly press coverage. He had begun very early in his Phoenix office chairing by video hookup a three-hour ICANN security meeting, all the while scanning his email, where members of the Cabal were posting links to the mounting hilarity. Rodney flew to San Francisco later that day to give a talk, and spent the cocktail hour portion of the event railing against idiot journalists.

At his suburban New Jersey home office, Andre DiMino experienced the day as another coup for the botmaster, who had made them all look foolish. Andre had given an interview the day before to NBC reporters for a segment to air on the *Today Show,* dressed in a green T-shirt with a mike hanging from the collar, cautioning the reporter (who didn't have a clue what he was talking about) that the botnet might not actually do anything big the next morning, that it might just generate all these new domain names and begin looking for instructions; but then he could see the Glaze descend. What could he do about the journalists' love of doomsday predictions, and their utter lack of technical proficiency, not to mention their lack of subtlety? His cautionary words slipped off into the ether, sandwiched between the trumpets of impending doom.

Still, Andre had kept his eye on his monitors through most of the day . . . *just in case.*

Very early in the morning, in his Alexandria office, big Dre Ludwig was not letting this get him down. He had been up all night and was feeling self-congratulatory, and a little tipsy. He wrote to the List:

My thoughts are as follows.
1. This has been an amazing effort from the very start on both a technical and logistical level.
2. We made HUGE political steps . . . and did what even governments could not effectively do.

3. Regardless of if we completely remove Conficker form the face of the globe WE STILL WALK AWAY WITH A HUGE WIN!

4. This is hopefully just an example of what WE can ALL do when we work together. Collaboration vs. Competition plain and simple, this is the first time that this has happened in the REGISTRY world. That alone is worth noting in my view, us security nerds have been banding together for years now to tackle threats. This has NEVER happened before in the registry (TLD) world, the closest thing we had was little islands (one or two) of registry operators who would actually take action. Even that has been a helluva battle for some of us to even get done these last few years.

This is in my own view of the fruition of years of work for me, so if you can't tell I'm more than a bit giddy. I blame the Scotch and time of morning as well!

Dre spent most of the day watching the List and various other chat channels, not really expecting to see anything happen, but aware of what might. The worst part of it for him still was not knowing what the botmaster had in mind. No one knew. Why had the worm been created, anyway?

Paul Vixie treated it like any other workday. He was in his San Francisco office early, confident that the worm was well confined, at least for the time being. At the very least they had made the botmaster *think*. Vixie's thoughts turned now to remediation. Time for the industry to wake up and begin fighting viruses directly, targeting infected machines with software designed to search and destroy malware. Clean up whole networks! Maybe Conficker had been the scare everyone needed. He was hopeful, though hopefulness was not his usual state.

Rick Wesson was also in his Mission District office, feeling pretty good about things, and giving lots of interviews. It was hard to believe all the press attention. He was tired. He had few illusions about their "victory," posting to the List:

> Nothing happened because our opponent is smart. They waited 2 months before they got the B => C update past me. We weren't even lucky. If the Conficker authors had wanted it they could have it tomorrow.
>
> Everyone deserves pats on the back, but the game isn't over . . . it just started.

John Crain was at home in Long Beach. He, too, watched the List throughout the day, but he assumed this would be the least likely day for the botmaster to make a move.

No matter how dismissive the rest of the world might be, the Cabal knew the threat was real, and would not go away. The botnet was still out there . . . biding its time. Still, as the days progressed and Conficker did nothing, they wondered. Had their effort with the TLDs entirely succeeded?

One week after C-Day, that question was answered. The botnet successfully received instructions, apparently via a peer-to-peer connection from a computer in South Korea, and for the first time since it was first spotted in November, the worm did something—something really stupid. It rented itself out for two weeks to a notorious spammer called Waledec.

This enormous botnet, this potential Internet-destroyer, leased itself out briefly to distribute one of the most pedestrian, well-known species of malware in the taxonomy. And the reaction was: *This is it?* It was like a bad joke. It was like that classic scene in *Spinal Tap* when, after a breathless buildup of the band's new Stonehenge theme, a replica of the ancient monument is dramatically lowered onstage, but the prop is only *knee high!* Or like the moment in an old circus clown act when the villain at last corners the hero, aims a huge pistol, pulls the trigger, and out pops a little flag displaying the word "BANG!"

Conficker spread Waledac for a few weeks, and then stopped.

What did it mean? For one thing, it demonstrated that the botnet was fully functional, fully capable of receiving instructions. The Cabal had apparently shut down access via a website, and this was an amazing accomplishment; but the botmaster performed a simple end run with his new peer-to-peer capability, just as Hassen had suspected when he first dissected the thing. It was taken by most in the Cabal as a message from their opponents. It said: *You know what? We know what we're doing. We can use this thing whenever we want.*

It meant, ultimately, that the enormous effort expended to tie up all those domain names through 116 separate TLD operators, every country code in the world, had failed.

It meant . . . *the worm won.*

Or did it?

It has now been more than two years since C-Day, or *Cybarmageddon*, and except for its little stunt with Waledec, the botnet has done nothing—at least nothing obvious. And remember the two signatures of modern war: (1) You never win, exactly; you *claim* victory. (2) Perception is paramount.

So what exactly had happened? The botnet was still out there, millions of bots automatically churning out domain names by the thousands, every day, week after week, month after month, year after year. The sinkhole monitors established by the Cabal still chart the activity day by day, hour by hour, minute by minute. The Conficker botnet, this enormous concentration of computer power, had been assembled and was still in the hands of its mysterious creators. Those machines were *pwned,* or owned, and they could be turned to any task the botmaster defined. They could be leased for plunder or marshaled for attack.

The Cabal had pulled off an impressive feat, dissecting the worm, coordinating an unprecedented global response, and setting up a dynamic, smoothly functioning system to monitor the botnet's data traffic and to sinkhole it. All of that work, the many thousands of hours, the considerable brainpower and experience, had been volunteer. There was no budget for it, beyond Rick Wesson's credit cards. And what had it earned them, beyond a sense of satisfaction and the admiration of their small group of peers? In the larger world, it had mostly earned ridicule. They were the guys who had (supposedly) claimed the sky was going to fall on April 1, 2009.

Of course, they hadn't, but that fact required more explanation than the nightly news was equipped to give. The government had been made somewhat more aware, and, curiously, would even declare victory! A Department of Homeland Security (DHS) "Lessons Learned" report, issued early in 2011, summed up the effort thus:

"In an unprecedented act of coordination and collaboration, the cybersecurity community, including Microsoft, ICANN, domain registry operators, anti-virus vendors, and academic researchers, organized to block the infected computers from reaching the domains—an informal group that was eventually dubbed the Conficker Working Group. They sought to register and otherwise block domains before the Conficker author, preventing the author from updating the botnet. Despite a few errors, the effort was very successful."

The key word there would be *very*, as opposed to *completely*. As Rick had pointed out again and again, *almost* doesn't cut it. All it takes is one successful link, like the peer-to-peer connection that prompted the Waledec stunt, and . . . game over. The upbeat DHS report was some kind of high-water mark for government gall—a tough record to beat. After sitting back and watching the Cabal do all the work, and nearly succeed, Uncle Sam finally found a role for himself: *proclaim victory and then stick a flag in it!*

It is a curious finding, given that Rodney, who has since become the official head of the Cabal (the very same Conficker Working Group celebrated in the report), has this to say about what happened:

"At the end of the day, it's a failure. It's a success as a model and an organization, but we actually don't have control over Conficker. We didn't achieve the objective."

This DHS report, it should be noted, was also the high-water mark for government involvement in the actual battle. On page 33 of the report itself, one unnamed member of the Cabal summed up the feds' contribution during the actual conflict:

"Zero involvement, zero activity, zero knowledge."

Nevertheless, the new administration seemed to get it. Behind a lectern in the East Room of the White House on May 30, 2009, President Barack Obama, who was just moving into the White House when the effort peaked, gave a speech about cybersecurity.

"We meet today at a transformational moment—a moment in history when our interconnected world presents us, at once, with great promise but also great peril." He called the nation's digital infrastructure "the backbone that underpins a prosperous economy and a strong military and an open and efficient government." Cyberspace is "real," he said, "and so are the risks that come with it."

He cited Conficker in particular to illustrate the feds' anemic capability to defend the Internet:

"It's . . . clear that we're not as prepared as we should be, as a government or as a country. . . . Just as we failed in the past to invest in our physical infrastructure—our roads, our bridges and rails—we've failed to invest in the security of our digital infrastructure. . . . Indeed, when it comes to cybersecurity, federal agencies have overlapping missions and don't coordinate and communicate nearly as well as they should—with each other or with the private sector. We saw this in the disorganized response to Conficker, the Internet 'worm' that in recent months has infected millions of computers around the world. This status quo is no longer acceptable—not when there's so much at stake. We can and we must do better."

Most members of the Cabal say that the government has gotten better. Some of its members have gone to work for government agencies. U.S. CERT's Mischel Kwon, whose performance the Cabal found singularly unimpressive, resigned just a few months after the president's remarks —Rodney suspects that the desperate repackaging of his Conficker PowerPoint by the agency played a role.

In Pittsburgh there is now the National Cyber-Forensics Training Alliance, a privately funded effort affiliated with Carnegie-Mellon University and modeled consciously after the Cabal, where federal agents work alongside industry researchers. This alliance has begun to make real progress training the kind of experts needed to deal with the growing malware threat.

"There are guys from Target and from eBay and from E*TRADE, and from other banks, who have full-time employees that are assigned there," says Rodney. "And when they're able to establish a case, they hand it across the desk to an agent who can now go and get an official case going. It's highly effective. The best bang for the buck in the entire federal government from a cybersecurity point of view."

In June 2011, the Pentagon announced that it was putting the finishing touches on a new strategy for dealing with cyberattacks. It will define any attack on important computer networks that leads to civilian casualties to be an act of aggression against the United States; this means that if it can be determined where the attack originated, the nation might respond in a variety of ways, including militarily. It was, however, more a statement of mounting concern than a blueprint for national defense.

"The policy says nothing about how the United States might respond to a cyberattack from a terrorist group or other nonstate actor," wrote *New York Times* reporters David E. Sanger and Elisabeth Bumiller. "Nor does it establish a threshold of what level of cyberattack merits a military response."

Despite the vagueness of the pronouncement, it became clear in July 2010 that malware was a serious weapon in the arsenals of great powers. Alarmed by a secret Iranian program to develop nuclear weapons, and the inability of international nonproliferation agreements to stop it, nations opposed to the effort (probably the United States or Israel, perhaps both) infected the computer networks in Iran's uranium enrichment plants with a worm dubbed Stuxnet. The worm employed the same buffer overflow exploit at Port 445 used by Conficker, penetrating Windows Operating Systems, and was tailored specifically to sabotage the centrifuges used to spin uranium at high speed in order to separate out weapons-grade isotopes. Pentrating a specific variety of software sold by the German engineering giant Seimans AG, the worm caused the centrifuges to spin wildly out of control, destroying the uranium processing facilities and setting back the Iranian effort for years. Even though Stuxnet infected a great many computers outside Iran, its careful design meant that it executed harmful instructions only on the Siemens AG software at the uranium processing plants. It was the first of what are likely to be many carefully sculptured cyberattacks, and clearly learned from the successful implementation of Conficker.

These kinds of tailored, targeted attacks were considered the trend in early 2011, as I finished writing this book.

Criminal attacks in recent weeks had successfully hit the International Monetary Fund, Google, Lockheed-Martin, Sony, and Citibank, among others. The difference between these and cyberthreats in the past, including Conficker, is that they do not spread indiscriminately on the Internet, and do not seek to assemble botnets, even though they may use existing botnets as a platform. They are the difference between a smart bomb and a conventional one: they zero in on specific targets and have narrowly defined goals. They illustrate once more the growing sophistication of criminals, spies, and military organizations, who remain every bit or more than a match for those who, like the Cabal, seek to preserve the Internet as a free zone for exchanging information and for commerce. This is one of the defining battles of our age, one that takes place for the most part out of the public eye.

Meanwhile, the Conficker botnet itself waits.

Most of those in the Cabal now doubt that it will ever be used. The theory here is that the Cabal's coordinated effort, while ultimately unable to kill the botnet, made it too hot to handle. Any move the botmaster makes might help identify him (or them), pinpoint him, bring the law down on him. This is a point of view that supports the claim of victory, albeit victory of a limited sort.

"Somebody got pissed that we shone a light down their hallway or in their bedroom or whatever," says Dre Ludwig. "I mean, realistically that's what it looks like. Too much attention. Too dangerous to play with anymore. And it demonstrated [how to mount an] effort, concerted effort, to mitigate it. If that thing ever fired up again we'd get the old band back together. It's been done once."

Others, like Andre DiMino of Shadowserver, are more inclined to believe that Conficker's controllers are simply biding their time.

"They are watching us watch them," he says. "I'm thinking that it's really either that somebody *let* this thing get bigger, or it's advanced bigger and farther than they ever dreamed possible. A lot of people think that. But in looking at the sophistication of this thing and looking at the evolution of this thing, I think they knew exactly what they were doing. I think they were trying something, and I think that they're too smart to do what everybody figured they were going to do. You have to remember, the world was watching this thing on April 1st, waiting for the world to end on April 1st. The last thing you'd want to do if you're the bad guy is make something happen then. You're going to wait until . . . say, May 28th of 2010, or, pick any other date, to do something. You're going to do something when you're least suspected. These guys are sophisticated. They have good code. And just even seeing the evolution from Conficker A to B to C . . . these guys know exactly what they're doing."

Rodney agrees, and more so. Just because no one has seen Conficker make a move, he says, doesn't mean that it has not.

"People are saying that Conficker is not really used for anything because it's not—it's just too visible. What's your point that it's too visible? How does a weapons platform become too visible? Do you mean that it's so visible that we know how to stop it? It's really hard to get rid of on infected machines. But [Conficker] has the Holy Grail of malware, which is something called stability. There are six million machines and tomorrow there will be six million machines, give or take. You can count on this botnet. What a botmaster wants always is to know that his machines are going to be up—that someone isn't going to take them down. This thing has proven . . . that it is rock-solid, and that the good guys, and the antivirus guys, and the Microsoft guys can't do shit. It is the Holy Grail of a botnet. So what we have in place is a weapons platform that's capable, and it's going to stay capable."

Rodney has a theory. Every day, on average, the botnet loses about half a million machines and gains another half million. The Cabal's researchers track this. Some machines disappear because they are turned off, wear out, or are replaced, and some because they are disinfected (the Cabal has distributed a free, easy-to-use tool to tell if a computer is infected). Others are added because the worm continues to spread via its peer-to-peer capability. But what if some of those machines that disappear vanish because the botmaster is selling off pieces of the botnet every day to criminal spammers?

It's plausible, because the botnet is valuable in any number of ways. It can be used to generate a great deal of computing power, or just as a known store of vulnerable machines to exploit. All of the machines on Conficker's lists have stopped receiving security updates.

"So when people say Conficker's doing nothing . . . I don't believe that," Rodney says. "We think it's doing nothing because we don't observe anything. But we don't know. And a perfect way for this group to actually be monetizing it in a way that just, like, generates revenue every day and would never be noticed, is by sending off targeted pieces to criminals of some kind. Whether they are a nation-state or just criminals selling off these small pieces [they] would just never be noticed. And I believe that's what's happening."

So while the Cabal may have pointed the way toward a cooperative defense against Internet threats, and may have smartened up the government a little, the worm itself survives. Both sides of the Conficker battle took away valuable lessons.

Paul Vixie has plenty of new material for his "Internet Rant," that speech he gives in his affectless monotone about the Internet as an example of "historical folly." His hope two years ago, the day Cybarmageddon didn't happen, was that after everyone got over the laugh, the Conficker scare might spur efforts toward remediation—a concerted effort to rid machines of the worm. That hope has been disappointed, and he is back to predicting doom.

He is also fed up with Microsoft. In a note to the List later in 2009, Vixie fingered what he believes is the heart of the problem:

> This whole thing is Microsoft's fault. Really. One company brought us Conficker. Stock symbol, MSFT. . . . The pink elephant in this living room is: Microsoft did this to us. I am not referring to Microsoft's continuing . . . monopoly by which they forced all kinds of end users and resellers to include Windows on the ten million computers now infected by Conficker. That's evil, and if I ever meet a space alien I will be ashamed for all of humanity at the way we herd our sheeple into pens and suck their blood in this way.

Paul pointed out that Microsoft had issued a patch years earlier dealing with exactly the same kind of vulnerability as the one at Port 445, but that the company's security software engineers had failed to check to see if the flaw existed elsewhere.

> What this means, gentlemen, is that some employee of Microsoft patched it in one place without patching it in the other place, even though they were both in the same source file. This means the employee who did the patch, and the reviewers, and the managers, and the QA [quality assurance] teams, for MS06-040, all had a chance to do a thorough review of the source module for any similar code sequence or vulnerability, and they *flubbed it*.

He concluded:

Yo, T.J., nothing personal, man.

T.J. has been busy. In the last two years, he has helped put together a cooperative Microsoft/law enforcement initiative that has taken down, with the help of the U.S. Marshal Service, Waledec and Rustock, two infamous spamming operations, targeting the servers that hosted the criminal enterprise. As a result, he says the company has seen at least a temporary decline in the amount of spam on the Internet.

The Conficker botmaster is still out there. In June of 2011, authorities in Ukraine, in cooperation with the FBI, arrested sixteen hackers in Kiev, who had reportedly used the Conficker botnet to drain $72 million from international banking accounts. The investigation was run out of the Seattle FBI office, the one which has worked closely with T.J., and was assisted by the National Cyber-Forensics Training Alliance. Servers in several countries were raided in a coordinated international police action. Those rounded up were all young men between the ages of twenty-six and thirty-three, who police said had "splendid technical educations." It remained doubtful, however, that among this group was the Conficker botmaster, the designer. More likely, these hackers were customers of the botnet's creator, using its stable platform to launch their targeted thievery, in exactly the way Harvard's Schecter and Smith predicted in their 2003 "Access for Sale" paper. Agents were still questioning the suspects as this book was going to press. There were hopes that this group might lead authorities to the botmaster, the true architect, or architects, of the worm. Rodney is optimistic, even confident on some days, that he, or they, will be caught.

More than a year after the anticlimactic April 1 Conficker stunt, Rodney, John Crain, Phil Porras, and Andre DiMino met with representatives from the White House in Rodney's Neustar office—it was the first time Phil had ever met Rodney personally. Paul Vixie added his gloomy perspective by phone hookup. Andre had prepared lists of Conficker infections on *.gov* and *.mil* networks. The scope of the worm's inroads clearly startled the Obama team. Rodney was particularly alarmed that here, more than a year after he had sounded the alarm on Capitol Hill, the Commerce Department, the government's chief computer network guardian, was still not tracking the infection closely itself.

At a follow-up meeting several months later, Andre says, CERT acquitted itself much better, and the infection rates on *.gov* and *.mil* had gone down significantly.

So who is the botmaster? Who are the bad guys behind the worm?

Ramses Martinez is in charge of security for VeriSign, the Dulles, Virginia, company that operates two of the root servers for the Internet. He was a member of the Cabal.

One of the things he does, patrolling the perimeter at VeriSign looking for threats, is occasionally dip into the obscure digital forums where cybercriminals converse, where those who write sophisticated malware boast and threaten and compare notes. After all, theirs is a rarefied community, and those engaged in this game have certainly encountered the Glaze themselves often enough. The chat rooms are a community of the like-minded, a place where they can show off their chops among those who appreciate their skills, where they can compare notes, learn. White hats like Ramses sometimes venture in to collect intelligence, or just out of curiosity, or for fun. Often they pretend to be malware creators themselves, but not always. Sometimes they enter as themselves, and indulge in a little cyber–trash talk.

"In the past you were just sort of making sure they didn't steal your database of credit cards," he says. "Now we go in to engage them. You talk to them and you exchange information. You have a guy in Russia selling malware working with a guy in Mexico doing phishing attacks that's talking to a kid in Brazil who's doing credit card fraud, and they're introducing each other to some guy in China doing something else."

Martinez said he recently eavesdropped on a dialogue between a security researcher and a man he suspects was at least partly responsible for Conficker. He won't say how he drew that connection; he says only that he had good reasons for believing it to be true. The suspect in the conversation was Russian. The standard image of a malevolent hacker is the Hollywood one, a brilliant twentysomething with long hair and a bad attitude, and in need of a bath.

This is not how Martinez sees him.

"I see him as a really well-educated, smart businessman," he says. "He may be fifty years old. These guys are not chumps. They're not just out to make a buck."

Ramses joined the conversation with this fellow. He made no effort to disguise himself. And when the Russian realized whom he was talking to, he quickly retreated from the conversation.

He wrote apologetically:

> You're the good guys; we're the bad guys. Bacillus can't live with antibodies.

. . . And, oh, one last thing: somebody still owes Rick Wesson $30,000.

SOURCES

INTERVIEWS

All of the principals in this story were generous with me in both sharing their stories and reviewing the manuscript for errors, particularly Phil Porras, Hassen Saidi, Andre DiMino, Rick Wesson, Rodney Joffe, and Dre Ludwig, who went above and beyond. I also interviewed James Bosworth, T. J. Campana, John Crain, Dave Dittrich, Barry Green, Brian Krebs, Chris Lee, Michael Ligh, John Markoff, Ramses Martinez, Richard Perlotto, Mike Reavey, Joe Stewart, Paul Twomey, and Paul Vixie. It would be hard to understate my knowledge of the Internet and of computer operations before I began, so it would be hard to overstate the patience these men demonstrated trying to explain things to me. Rick Wesson and Phil Porras shared their email archives, and the Cabal (the Conficker Working Group) voted me in so that I could access the thousands of emails on their Listserv. I still wish they had official caps and T-shirts so that I could advertise my honorary membership in the X-Men.

The Conficker Working Group archives are referred to

below as "CArchives," and Rick Wesson's and Phil Porras's personal email archives as "WArchives" and "PArchives," respectively. The books and articles cited in the story are itemized in the chapter notes that follow.

NOTES

CHAPTER 1: ZERO

New Mutant Activity Registered, "The Amazing X-Men, The Age of Apocalypse," Marvel Comics, April 1995; *The new worm . . . their own tribe,* Porras and Saidi; *They are mutants . . . normal humans,* "The Amazing X-Men," March 1995; The quote from *Computer Power and Human Reason* is from page 116 of the 1976 paperback W.H. Freeman edition; *Phil himself . . . rested on their work,* Wesson, Porras, and the CWG archives; *The world they inhabit . . . how it transmitted data,* drawn from *Where Wizards Stay Up Late,* by Katie Hafner and Matthew Lyon, Simon & Schuster Paperbacks, 1996, an excellent, highly readable early history of the Internet; *more than two billion users,* according to the U.N. Telecommunications Union, January 26, 2011; *Its growth has been . . . nanosecond to nanosecond,* Porras, Crain; *. . . visual illustration . . . Bar Elan University,* as reported in *Technology Review,* June 19, 2007; *Behind his array . . . worm's purpose,* Porras; *Phil had no way to stop . . . us to do,* Porras.

CHAPTER 2: MS08-067

The world is no Longer yours, "The X-Men Chronicles," Marvel Comics, 1995; *The first reports . . . this one,* Campana; *Gates and Paul Allen . . . and the European Commission,* Most of the summary history of Microsoft is drawn from *Hard Drive: Bill Gates and the Making of the Microsoft Empire,* a good early history of Gates and the organization by James Wallace and Jim Erickson; *unfair and monopolistic,* In the April 3, 2000 judgment in *Microsoft v. the U.S.,* an antitrust case brought by the U.S. Department of Justice, the corporation was called "an abusive monopoly." Microsoft settled the case with the U.S. Department of Justice in 2004. In March of the same year the European Union brought an antitrust case against Microsoft that resulted in a $613 million judgment against Gates's corporation; *Many geeks . . . share of the market,* Vixie, Wesson, DiMino, Ludwig, Porras there is evidence for Microsoft's claim that it is most-targeted because it is large. As Apple's share of the market has grown in recent years, so has its share of problems with malware, see http://www.betancws.com/article/Apples-Mac-Detender-patch-is-already-worthless/ 1306953026; *. . . the size of the Redmond campus . . . of the interface,* Microsoft. I visited the Redmond campus in 2010 to meet with Campana, and my descriptions of the place here and earlier are drawn from that visit; *He does not look like . . . less sophisticated crooks,* Campana, Porras, DiMino, Porras; *In September 2008 . . . the lock had been picked,* Campana, Porras, Saidi, Reavey; *T.J. and his team . . . it just made things worse,* Campana, DiMino, Stewart, Porras; *"If the bad people . . . wreak havoc,"* Sites quoted in *USA Today's*

"Technology Live," October 23, 2008, "Microsoft Issues Security Patch for Giant Hole," by Michelle Kessler; *Twenty-eight days . . . Campana*; Campana.

CHAPTER 3: REMOTE THREAD INJECTION

"If he came here . . . imagine, sir," "The Amazing X-Men," Marvel Comics, March 1995; *Hassen Saidi . . . burn it down,* Saidi; *At the down . . . more ambitious,* Stewart, Joffe; *Cyberattacks were launched,* For more on cyberattacks in Estonia see the BBC report from May 17, 2007, "Cyber Raiders Hitting Estonia," http://news.bbc.co.uk/2/hi/europe/6665195.stm; For Georgia attacks see the *Washington Post*'s Brian Krebs, October 16, 2008, "Russian Hacker Forums Fueled Georgia Cyber Attacks," http://voices.washingtonpost.com/securityfix/2008/10/report_russian_hacker_forums_f.html; For more on Stuxnet see the *New York Times* report by William J. Broad, John Markoff, and David Sanger, January 15, 2011, "Israeli Test on Worm Called Crucial in Iran Nuclear Delay," http://www.nytimes.com/2011/01/16/world/middleeast/16stuxnet.html?_r=1&ref=siemensag; For more on the Zeus Trojan see the *New York Times* story by John Markoff, February 18, 2010, "Malicious Sostware Infects Computers," http://www.nytimes.com/2010/02/19/technology/19cyber.html?scp=8&sq=Zeus%20Trojan&st =Search; *The stakes are high maddeningly literal,* Porras, Saidi; *Bill Gates . . . precise statements,* "Programmers at work" intr. can be found at http://programmersatwork.wordpress.com/bill-gates-1976; *Say, for instance . . . protect its communications,* Porras, Saidi; *Breaking*

codes . . . not be able to decode it, The Code Book, by Simon Singh, Anchor Books, 1999, pages 268–79; *This meant . . . botnet to last,* Saidi; *Huge amounts of money,* The report by Brian Krebs, "Massive Profits Fueling Rogue Antivirus Market," was published March 16, 2009, http://voices.washingtonpost. com/securityfix/2009/03/obscene_profits_fuel_rogue_ant. html; *At first glance . . . getting started;* Porras, Saidi. There remain alternative accounts of how Conficker got its name, but this one sounded the most plausible to me. I have also heard that the name was coined by researchers at F-Secure, but it seems clear that its origin is rooted in *TrafficConverter.biz,* the first malware contact made by the worm when it initiated.

CHAPTER 4: AN OCEAN OF SUCKERS

Having mutant powers . . . others, "The X-Men Chronicles," March 1995; *The idea . . . it's a neat bit of work, The Shockwave Rider,* John Brunner, Harper & Row, 1975, page 222; Reference to *Future Shock* as a source is on the Acknowledgments page of *Shockwave Rider; The Cuckoo's Egg,* by Cliff Stoll, Pocket Books, 2005; *The idea was called . . . surviving nodes, Where the Wizards Stay Up Late,* pages 54–66; My account of the evolution of Conficker comes primarily from interviews with Stewart, DiMino, and Porras, with specifics of the individual viruses and worms from Wikipedia entries for each. Wikipedia, while an unreliable source for many things, is, perhaps unsurprisingly, a comprehensive and reliable source for information about computers, computer history, and malware; *The next step . . . such an intrusion,* "Access for Sale," Schecter and Smith, 2003.

CHAPTER 5: THE X-MEN

He and others . . . for being gifted, "The X-Men Chronicles," Marvel Comics, March 1995; *By mid-December . . . on the Internet,* infection numbers were being tracked primarily by Shadowserver and by Wesson at this point. The number reflects calls to command and control locations from different IP addresses, as they arrived at the various sinkholes. Efforts were made to avoid counting more than once a computer sending multiple messages; *Beyond this group . . . down the line,* Hruska's article can be found at arstechnica.com/security/news/2008/12/time-for-forced-updates-conficker-botnet-makes-us-wonder.ars; *In the case of . . . effort against Conficker,* Vixie. A video of his Defcon 13 speech can be found at http://www.youtube.com/watch?v=wP5TQlaWiuE; *"Private sector . . . paralyze the United States,"* p. 165. The full report can be found at http://www.uscc.gov/annual_report/2008/annual_report_full_08.pdf; *The ad hoc group . . . over their heads,* Joffe, Porras, Wesson, DiMino, Ludwig, et al.; *We are the last line . . . if not now . . . when?* Conficker Archives 2/9/09; *Shades of Samuel Richardson,* *"Whenever I'm added . . . the suspense,"* CArchives. 3/2/09; *"I feel like . . . high school,"* WArchives 2/20/09; *By the end of . . . melting completely,"* Campana.

CHAPTER 6: DIGITAL DETECTIVES

This may not be . . . fight for it, "The Amazing X-Men, Age of Apocalypse," April 1995; *At the October . . . hard to believe,* Campana, DiMino; *Brian Krebs . . . even respond,* DiMino.

Krebs's article, "Bringing Botnets Out of the Shadows," March 21, 2006, can be found at http://www.washingtonpost.com/wp-dyn/content/article/2006/03/21/AR2006032100279.html; *Gratitude started . . . begin to stop it?* DiMino; *No one was deeper . . . command center,* Porras, Twomey, DiMino; *Finding that . . . government agencies,* Porras, Saidi; *Phil needed . . . back of his hand,* Wesson; *The Internet, unlike roads . . . to that domain;* Wesson, Joffe, DiMino; *At a time . . . Internet security,* Wesson; *So when Phil . . . for the suggestion,* Porras, first quote from PArchives 12/15/08, exchange with U.S. CERT, PArchives 12/15/08; *Setting aside . . . just 12,292),* Wesson, CArchives 12/29/08; *There were . . . nation-state,* Porras, Wesson, Joffe, DiMino; *China was . . . overall strategy,* 2008 U.S.-China Security Review, both quotes from page 165; *Those who . . . wake-up call?* Joffe, Wesson; *When Chris Lee . . . source for the worm!* Lee; *Meanwhile, Phil . . . tripping over each other,* PArchives, 12/21/08; Dagon would become a central player in the Cabal.

CHAPTER 7: A NOTE FROM THE TRENCHES

All the training . . . put to the test, "The X-Men Chronicles," Marvel Comics, March 1995; *T. J. Campana's birthday . . . ruined his birthday,* Campana, Wesson; *For one thing . . . registered in China,* Joffe, Porras; *While the new variant . . . far enough,* Porras, Saidi, Joffe; *Particularly troubling . . . 8.9 million,* Porras, Joffe, Wesson. The F-Secure report can be found at http://www.f-secure.com/weblog/archives/archive-012009.html; *The level of sophistication*

. . . were pros, Porras, Saidi; *In Phoenix . . . a good one,* Joffe; *Phil agreed . . . opening for me,* Porras, Wesson, WArchives 1/30/09; *T.J. began . . . "We'll do the right thing,"* Campana, Joffe; *Just as the Cabal . . . on the horizon,"* Hruska's Ars Technica article can be found at http://arstechnica.com/security/ news/2009/01/conficker-worm-spikes-infects-1-1-million-pcs-in-24-hours.ars, and Markoff's January 22, 2009, *New York Times* article at http://www.nytimes.com/2009/01/23/ technology/internet/23worm.html?scp=1&sq=Markoff%20 new%20digital%20plague&st=cse; *Rick was not exaggerating . . . nature of the threat,* Wesson, both emails from WArchives 1/31/2009; *The Defense Intelligence official . . . don't call us,* Wesson. Woodcock's email is from WArchives 2/1/2009; *Out in Menlo Park . . . then nothing happened,* Porras.

CHAPTER 8: ANOTHER HUGE WIN

Remember . . . ALWAYS! "The X-Men Chronicles," Marvel Comics, March 1995; *So far the effort . . . to crumble,* DiMino, Joffe, Wesson, Ludwig; *So when . . . almighty dollar,* Ludwig, DiMino. Campana email from CArchives 2/7/2009, Ludwig and Campana emails from CArchives 2/3/09; *The Atlanta conference . . . swift response,* Joffe, Campana, Twomey, Crain, DiMino, Wesson; *With typical enthusiasm . . . see them,* Ludwig email CArchives 2/8/09; *There was such . . . good guys,* Ludwig, DiMino; *Whatever the title . . . it happens,* Ludwig email is from CArchives 2/24/09, FBI agent quote from Joffe; *It was typical . . . Rick was concerned,* Wesson; *Unfortunately, many . . . against it?* Ludwig, DiMino; *Dre Ludwig, in particular . . . do to Dre?* Ludwig, DiMino, Lee, Wesson; *Andre, ever . . . done before,* DiMino. The quoted Ludwig email is from WArchives 1/31/09; *Rick denied . . . like betrayal,* Ludwig, DiMino, Joffe, Wesson, Vixie; *Dre posted . . . right people's ears,* Ludwig email from CArchives 2/20/09; *On a sunny day . . . cloud of suspicion,* Wesson, Vixie; *Despite these . . . analyze them,* gleaned from February traffic on CArchives; *What they had . . . WIN!* Campana email from CArchives 2/4/09; *Dripping with . . . that goal,* Wesson email from CArchives 2/4/09; *Toni Koivunen . . . sits there?* Email from WArchives 1/23/09; *Rick wrote . . . economic goals,* WArchives 1/23/09; *If you're on the highway,* Conficker poem can be found at http://it.slashdot.org/story/09/02/20/239229/New-Conficker-Variant-Increases-Its-Flexibility; *Markoff called . . . time bomb,"* Markoff, *New York Times,* February 14, 2009, "Do We Need a New Internet?" can be found at http://www.nytimes.com/2009/02/15/weekinreview/15markoff.html?scp=1&sq=Markoff%20ticking%20time%20bomb&st=cse.

CHAPTER 9: MR. JOFFE GOES TO WASHINGTON

Today a massive . . . reality, "The X-Men Chronicles," Marvel Comics, March 1995; *Greetings to all . . . new variant,* CArchives, 3/6/09; *Phil Porras got . . . help fight it,* Porras, PArchives 3/6/09; *The really bad news . . . instead of 250,* CArchives 3/6/09; *F&*king hell . . . for Washington,* Joffe, all emails from CArchives, 3/6/09; *Rodney packed . . . eased with this information,* Joffe, Porras, Saidi; *Rick wrote . . . accurately,* WArchives, 3/7/09; *So on the same weekend . . . quantify the* *risk?* Joffe, CArchives 3/9–12/09; *It led to . . . eight days away,* CArchives, 3/14/09.

CHAPTER 10: CYBARMAGEDDON

And is it . . . the entire world? "The Amazing X-Men, Age of Apocalypse," Marvel Comics, April 1995; *John Crain . . . daily list,* Crain; *I do not have . . . Dre Ludwig,* CArchives, 3/16/09; *The botmaster was . . . on the subject,* Crain, Joffe, Lee; *When one of . . . on fire!* CArchives; *The Cabal set . . . wrote back to Chris,* Crain, CArchives; *I believe . . . added stress,* all emails from the CArchives; *Rick kicked up . . . pick up the phone,* WArchives 3/18/09; *When I operate . . . to be friends again,* WArchives 3/18/09; *It is my humble . . . cold hard data,* CArchives, 3/19/09; *I am growing tired . . . so pipe down,* WArchives 3/19/09; *Finally, T. J. Campana . . . agreed to behave,* Campana, Joffe, Wesson, Vixie. Campana and Joffe emails from WArchives 3/19/09; *John and Rick . . . the message got distorted,* Crain, Wesson, Joffe, DiMino; *Again it was . . . stirring things up,* Markoff, Wesson, Porras. The article, *New York Times,* March 18, 2009, "Computer Experts Unite to Hunt Worm," can be found at http://www.nytimes.com/2009/03/19/technology/19worm.html?scp=1&sq=Markoff%20devastating%20attack&st=cse; *On the last night . . . really it?* The *60 Minutes* report can be seen at http://www.youtube.com/watch?v=Ar-l3FRUdGw; *An Unthinkable Disaster?* 3/19/09. In fairness, though, as we know, blurbs seldom are fair, the full headline reads: "The Conficker Worm: April Fools' Joke or Unthinkable Disaster?"; *A Threat That Could . . . Entire Internet,* from the *60 Minutes* report; *A Deadly Threat, London Guardian,* 3/30/09. Again, in fairness, the complete headline reads: "Conficker Virus Could Be Deadly Threat or April Fools' Joke"; *Rodney had . . . wildly right,* Joffe.

CHAPTER 11: APRIL FOOLS

X-Men, our day has come, "The X-Men Chronicles," Marvel Comics, March 1995; *disaster warnings . . . sheep,* MWBlog, 4/1/09. The post can be found at http://www.teamfurry. com/wordpress/2009/04/01/breaking-news-conficker-became-self-aware/; *Wired . . . Me First,* Wired, 4/1/09. The post can be found at http://www.teamfurry.com/ wordpress/2009/04/01/breaking-news-conficker-became-self-aware/; *But the prospect . . . turning back,* Joffe, DiMino, Ludwig, Wesson, Porras, Crain; *Some of . . . anything,* WSJ Blogs. These can be seen at http://blogs.wsj.com/ digits/2009/03/26/conficker-dont-believe-the-hype/; *John Markoff of . . . Markoff didn't come,* Markoff, Porras; *Three hours . . .giant raspberry?* Joffe, DiMino. The email is from CArchives, 4/1/09; *At his suburban . . . just in case,* DiMino; *Very early . . . created anyway?* Ludwig, email from CArchives 4/1/09; *Paul Vixie . . . usual state,* Vixie; *Rick Wesson . . . just started,* Wesson, email from CArchives 4/1/09; *John Crain . . . a move,* Crain; *One week . . . the worm won,* Joffe, Wesson, DiMino, Ludwig, Porras, Crain; *Of course . . . zero knowledge,* "The Conficker Working Group: Lessons Learned" can be found online at http:// www.confickerworkinggroup.org/wiki/uploads/Conficker_ Working_Group_Lessons_Learned_17_June_2010_final.pdf.

The first quote is from page ii in the Executive Summary; *It is a . . . the objective,* Joffe; *Nevertheless . . . do better,* President Obama's complete remarks of May 29, 2009, can be found at http://projects.washingtonpost.com/obama-speeches/speech/317/; *Most members . . . point of view,* Joffe; *In June 2011 . . . military response,* from *New York Times,* May 31, 2011, "Pentagon to Concider Cyberattacks Acts of War." This can be found at http://www.nytimes.com/ 2011/06/01/us/politics/01cyber.html?_r=1&scp=1&sq=cyber%20security%20military%20response&st=cse; *Despite the vagurness . . . implementation of Conficker,* Joffe, and the *New York Times* report by William J. Broad, John Markoff, and David Sanger, January 15, 2011, "Israeli Test on Worm Called Crucial in Iran Nuclear Delay," http://www.nytimes.com/2011/01/16/world/middleeast/16stuxnet.html?_r=1&ref=siemensag; This whole thing, the Vixie email is from CArchives 1/19/10; *T.J. has been . . . spam on the Internet,* Campana; *More than a year . . . gone down significantly,* Joffe, DiMino, Porras; *Ramses Martinez . . . antibodies,* Martinez; *And, oh . . . $30,000,* Wesson.

GLOSSARY

Application (or App) – Computer software designed to help a user perform a certain function on the computer, whether word processing, drawing a picture, charting their blood pressure, etc.

ARPA – The Advanced Research Projects Agency, a remarkable civilian unit at the Pentagon in the 1960s devoted to cutting-edge research projects, where the idea for the Internet was hatched.

AV Vendor – An anti-virus vendor, a for-profit security company that markets software and data to protect computers and networks.

Bit – A single digit. In computer code, it would either be represented as a "0" or a "1."

Bot – Short for "robot," a computer that has been joined to an illicit network under outside control.

Botnet – a network of bots, or robot computers.

Byte – A unit of information in computer language that usually consists of eight digits, or bits.

DDoS Attack – A Dedicated Denial-of-Service attack, overwhelming a targeted server, or website, with such a flood of requests for response that it can force it to crash.

Domain – An address on the Internet, rendered in letters or numbers. The actual address of the website consists of strings of ones and zeroes; the Domain Name is meant in most cases to make the owner easily recognizable to a human being – i.e. *amazon.com*, or *google.com*. Domain Names are sold by Registries, who assign and protect them, making sure that no one but the paying customers can use them. Most Domains are represented on the Internet by websites, but not all.

Domain Name Algorithm (DNA) – The mathematical equation used by the worm to generate seemingly random lists of Domain Names, a technique to hide the location of the botnet's controller.

Dynamic Link Library (DLL) – This is the method Microsoft programmers employ to enable computers to exchange data.

Exploit – A program designed to break into an operating system by exploiting a flaw in its programming code. Increasingly, exploits have become vehicles for malware. They are marketed openly, and used by criminals to insert whatever malware they wish into targeted computers.

Firewall – Software that blocks unauthorized access to a computer or network while permitting authorized communications.

GeoIP – A service provided by *maxmind.com* which tells you where specific IP addresses are located in the real world.

Hash Algorithm – A carefully-defined mathematical method of detecting content modification. It will detect a single alteration of a binary message (written in ones and zeroes), even if the messages contains trillions of bits.

Honeynet – a network of virtual computers created by researchers to snare and study malware.

Honeypot – A computer, usually virtual, without any security safeguards, in other words, *designed* to be infected by malware.

HTTP – HyperText Transfer Protocol, the foundation of data communication for the World Wide Web.

Interface Manager – A layer of software between the operating system and an application that enables the user to move easily between functions, or run more than one simultaneously. Windows is an Interface Manager.

IP Address – short for "Internet Protocol Address," the ID number assigned to a specific computer in a network. Under the original IP Version 4, it consists of a 32-bit number. The newest version, being implemented gradually to accommodate the phenomenal growth of the Internet, uses a 128-bit number.

IRC Channel – Internet Relay Chat Channel, one of the oldest ways of setting up a forum on the Internet, where members of a group can communicate with each other either directly or broadcast messages to the entire group.

IRC Channels were the first employed to create and control botnets.

ISP – Internet Service Provider, a company or machine that connects individual computers or networks to the Internet.

IT – Information Technology.

IDN – Short for Internet Domain Name.

Kernel – The innermost core of a computer operating system.

Malware – short for "malicious software," any program designed to illicitly enter a computer and disable, damage or hijack its operations.

Object Code – The most basic language for computers, composed exclusively of the ones and zeroes of binary communications.

Peer-to-Peer Protocol (P2P) – Software than enables individual computers on a network to communicate and share data directly, without routing it through a central location. This was a critical innovation in Conficker C.

Port Mirror – A network configuration that automatically copies all data traffic at a particular port to a monitoring station, allowing security technicians to watch for intrusions.

Patch – A security update that fixes a flaw in the operating system that, in effect, plugs a newly-discovered hole in the computer's defenses.

Pwned – "owned," in the sense that your computer has been infected with a worm that gives an outside operator control over it. It is an awkward coinage, an example of puckish hacker humor: Geeks are notoriously bad spellers, and someone early on in the malware wars had typed a "p" instead of an "o" in typing out the word "owned." It stuck.

Registrar – An ICANN accredited company or organization that is authorized to provide registration services for the top-level domains such as *.com*, *.org* and *.net*. Registrars have contractual agreements with their customers. A Registrar submits all newly registered domains into the Registry.

Registry – A company or organization that maintains a centralized registry database for the Top-Level Domains. Currently there is only one Registry for every Top-Level domain, *.com*, *.org* and *.net*. NSI Registry maintains this Registry.

Remote Thread – Hidden code that executes itself within the virtual address space of an existing, legitimate process, in other words, a program that runs concurrent with another, so that it is not easily recognized even by a skilled technician looking for it.

Root Servers – Computers that function as the trunk lines for the Internet, managing traffic flow worldwide. There are 13 of them, labeled A, B, C, D … to M. Ten are in the United States, one each in Great Britain, Japan, and Sweden.

RPC (Remote Procedure Call) – A technology that allows a computer program to cause a subroutine or procedure to execute in another address space, usually on another computer or on a shared network, without the programmer explicitly coding the details for this remote interaction. This is what Conficker enabled on victimized computers.

Server – A computer program designed to coordinate the flow of data within linked computers, or between networks, such as connecting a corporate website or individual computer to the Internet.

Services.exe – A file in Windows that runs background applications, routine computer functions that do not ordinarily come to the attention of a user.

Service Pack Two – The 2004 Microsoft update that substantially changed the character of the operating system to regard any incoming data as a threat. A milestone in protecting computers from malware.

Sinkhole – A destination for data housed securely within a security network, in other words, a deliberate dead-end; the Cabal created several sinkholes to collect inquiries from Conficker bots to prevent them from successfully contacting the botmaster. The sinkhole also enabled the Cabal to count the number of infected machines and networks, and to know exactly where they were.

Source Code – Any of the various computer languages designed to render object code, the basic computer language of ones and zeroes, into something more intelligible.

Svchost.exe – Short for "Service Host," a file in Windows that directs incoming data to the appropriate location for it to run.

Top Level Domain (TLD) – A broad category for Domain Names – i.e. *.com*, *.biz*, *.edu*, etc. – that serve as a primary routing service for Internet traffic.

Unpack – To break through or strip away the deceptive coding that compresses and protects a malicious program.

Virtual computer – An operating system inside a large computer designed to function as a singular smaller one.

Virus – A form of malware that relies on human help to invade a computer, such as clicking unadvisedly on an unsolicited email attachment, or inserting an infected floppy disk or thumb drive into a vulnerable computer.

Waledec – A form of malware that threatens the victim with the loss of computer function if they do not download remedial software, which is fake.

Website – A user-friendly platform designed to serve as a visible and interactive Internet platform, or a virtual headquarters, for a Domain.

World Wide Web – is a system of interlinked hypertext documents (documents embedded with links to other, related content) accessed via the Internet.

Worm – A form of malware that spreads by itself; it does not require the computer user to do anything.